365

QUICK & EASY TIPS

HOME ORGANIZATION

QUICK & EASY TIPS

HOME ORGANIZATION

Simple Techniques to Keep Your Home
Neat and Tidy Year Round

weldon**owen**

CONTENTS

KITCHEN

PANTRY

DINING AREA

ENTRYWAY

LIVING ROOM

KIDS' ROOM

CLOSET

QUICK TIP: *Repel Bugs*

KIDS' CLOSET

LINEN CLOSET

BATHROOM

OFFICE

QUICK TIP: *Track Your Taxes*

QUICK TIP: *Binder It*

CAR

OUTDOOR

QUICK TIP: *Use the Perimeter*

GARAGE

QUICK TIP: *Store Tools*

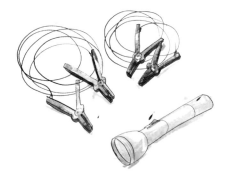

KITCHEN

001 REINVENT YOUR KITCHEN

The kitchen is the heart of the home, and a well-planned space will streamline food prep, cooking, baking, and cleaning—all while maximizing time and efficiency. Before you start pulling everything out of the cabinets and drawers, begin by writing out a plan. A plan will help you focus on what needs to be done. Consider how many cabinets and drawers you have. What needs organizing? Which areas are used for which tasks? How many gadgets, small appliances, and dishes can you purge, and how much space will result? Once you've got your guidelines, it's time to get started.

002

THINK ABOUT YOUR KITCHEN IN ZONES

Consider what you need from each space in your kitchen. Create zones for cooking, cleaning, dish storage, food storage, and food preparation. You know better than anyone where you need to keep essentials and what your workspaces are. Set them up accordingly to cut down on time spent searching for things while you're cooking.

003

CREATE STATIONS

Consider creating stations around your kitchen to make it easy and fun for you and your guests to enjoy the space. Create stations based on your own routines—consider a breakfast bar, a coffee bar, a granola or oatmeal station, or even a cocktail or mocktail bar.

004
CRAFT A
COOKING SPACE

The area around the stove and the adjacent countertop should accommodate cooking. Knives, cutting boards, and your prep area should all be located nearby so you're not crisscrossing the kitchen searching for tools and ingredients. Keep frequently used spices, oils, vinegars, and other seasonings handy (but not so close to the stove that they're damaged by its heat). Your nicest condiments and seasonings will be reserved for special meals, so they can be stored farther away in the pantry.

005
STAY
SPICY

Spices are the heart (and heat) of any home-cooked meal, and storing them effectively will make your cooking more enjoyable. Create a spice station to organize seasonings, oils, and spice blends. Whether you use matching containers or a hodgepodge of bottles and jars, make sure your spices are stored in containers that are airtight, see-through, and clearly labeled with expiration dates. (Toss out expired spices and condiments—their flavor won't last.) To make it easy to find what you need, consider sorting by size, type of item, most-used combinations, or savory, spicy, and sweet applications.

006

TIGHTEN YOUR KITCHEN TOOLBELT

Be judicious when choosing which kitchen tools you keep or toss. Eliminate duplicates and single-use gadgets that collect dust at the back of the drawer or cabinet. The same goes for other kitchen accessories. If it's stained, broken, or just unnecessary, get rid of it or set it aside for donation.

007

EDIT YOUR PREP ZONE

Take inventory of the supplies and appliances you use most often while prepping food and designate a place for the items most frequently in rotation. Keep cutting boards, knives, bowls, and other prepping essentials organized and easy to find nearby. Like your spice station (Item 005), this area should be close to the stove so you can keep an eye on what's cooking.

008 CORRAL CLEANING SUPPLIES

It's easy to let cleaning supplies pile up in your under-the-sink cabinet. The easiest way to bring order to the chaos? Use clear plastic bins to create caddies for different tasks. Dishes get a container with dishwasher pods, gloves, extra dish soap, sponges, and a scrubber. Surface cleaners, rags, microfiber cloths, and disinfectants can be stored together. Storing items in ready-to-go bins makes it easier to see what you're missing, and you can grab the whole bin and bring it wherever you need.

QUICK TIP

SNEAK IN UNDER-SINK SHELVING

If you have the bandwidth for an easy DIY project, consider adding shelves to your under-the-sink cabinet. Pull-out sliding shelves will double your storage while keeping everything close at hand.

009 BUILD YOUR OWN PANTRY

Not every home has a built-in pantry cabinet, but not to worry. You can dedicate a standing cabinet to store shelf-stable snacks and ingredients. Shelf expanders and stackable bins will help you make the most of the space you have. And don't obsess over having a Pinterest-perfect pantry—rather than splurging on matching glass storage containers, you'll be better off focusing on the storage you actually need, however mismatched your containers may be.

QUICK TIP

REUSE JARS

Instead of spending money on brand-new uniform glass containers, reuse glass jars and bottles with clean lids. If the mismatched lids bother you, cover them with craft paint or cloth. You won't waste money on containers you won't use, and you'll be able to source and replace jars as you need them.

010 STOW RARELY USED DISHES

If you have multiple dishware collections, consider keeping just one set of everyday dishes in your precious kitchen cabinet space. A shelf in a dining area or a credenza in the living room can show off everything else. If you have open shelving, use it to store large dishes that you use frequently. A decorative bowl might look beautiful on an open shelf, but if you never use it, it will end up collecting dust and grime.

011 END YOUR DAY WITH A CLEAN KITCHEN

Few things feel better than waking up to a clean space. At the end of each day, when dinner is done, take fifteen minutes to give everything a quick cleanup and wipe down: load and run the dishwasher (and empty it the next morning); clean the sink with a DIY cleaning solution (see Item 013); spray and wipe down the countertops, stovetops, table, and other surfaces; put a clean washcloth and dish towel out and toss the dirty ones in the laundry; and take the garbage out and put a new liner in the can. You'll notice that these easy tasks affect your mood for the rest of the evening—and make heading into the next day's meal preparations a breeze.

012 KEEP YOUR KITCHEN TIDY

Designate fifteen minutes a day to tidy your kitchen. Follow these steps:

☐ Wash any dishes that are in the sink.

☐ Put away anything that doesn't belong in the kitchen, on the counters or out in the open.

☐ Wipe down bottles and cartons that go from the table back to the fridge or pantry. This will prevent sticky messes and other surprise spills.

☐ Sweep up crumbs and wipe down any floor spills—this will make a deep clean much easier when the time comes.

013 MAKE A DIY SINK CLEANER

Some studies state a higher concentration of bacteria can be found in the kitchen sink than in the toilet bowl. Here's a recipe for an easy kitchen sink cleaner that you can DIY and use on a daily basis to keep the germs away.

YOU'LL NEED
- 1 clean spray bottle
- 1 part white vinegar
- 1 part water

DIRECTIONS
Mix the vinegar and water, cap your bottle, and shake vigorously. Use a permanent marker to label it "Daily Sink Cleaner"— this will prevent confusion with other sprays and remind you of its usefulness! Simply spray your sink and faucet, let sit for a few minutes, then wipe down. You'll have a fresher sink in no time.

014

BEHOLD THE MIGHTY MICROFIBER

One of the best ways to clean your counters is with warm water and a microfiber cloth. You never have to worry about your counter type, and the microfibers collect more dust, dirt, and even germs and bacteria than an old-school rag. They're effective enough to clean using just warm water, so you don't need abrasive chemical cleaners that could damage your countertops. To keep them feeling brand new, wash microfiber cloths in a separate load of laundry.

QUICK TIP

USE BAKING SODA AND LEMON

Baking soda may be the unsung hero of keeping your home fresh and clean. To make an easy pantry-sourced compound, use half of a lemon with some baking soda to create an abrasive scrubber. This combo also works on porcelain tub rust stains and many other seemingly tough cleaning jobs. The lemon has an added benefit of whitening areas that are yellowed. You'll be surprised how easily—and naturally—the markings lift off.

015 GO PORTABLE

Save time at breakfast or dinner by corralling your family's favorite condiments on a decorative tray. You can easily move the whole tray from the kitchen to the table and back: Gone are the days of searching for a stray pepper shaker while your eggs go cold. Common essentials include sugar, butter, olive oil, salt, and pepper, but prioritize whatever gets used the most!

016 RESTORE ORDER TO YOUR GADGET DRAWER

You know what they say: It's only helpful if you can find it. Assess the contents of your gadget drawer and consider whether you can use drawer dividers or compartments to keep tools organized. You can categorize by use, size and shape, or cooking versus baking. Don't forget to toss duplicates!

017 SECLUDE SHARP OBJECTS

Nobody wants an unexpected cut on their finger when they're busy looking for a ladle. Consider keeping sharp-edged kitchen tools, such as knives, can openers, peelers, mandolin slicers, and even pizza wheels in a separate drawer. If you have young kids, you'll want to store sharp tools out of reach.

018 MAKE KNIVES WORK

Your knives are one of your most important kitchen utensils, so you should store them carefully. A countertop knife block keeps knives protected and easily accessible, but it may not be worth the investment if you lack the counter space. If you have ample cabinet space, consider an in-drawer knife block. If you're short on kitchen space altogether, consider a wall-mounted magnetic knife strip. It keeps your knives visible, accessible, and out of the way.

019

KEEP FAVORITE UTENSILS HANDY

If you have a set of favorite stirrers or scrapers, make sure they're close by. Try storing them in a cute flowerpot or vintage cookie jar to give your counter a little unexpected flair.

020

SEPARATE LIDS FROM BASES

Whether you prefer plastic or glass, most food storage containers consist of two pieces: the base and the lid. Gain control of this area by storing lids separately, in a designated basket or tucked inside a hanging door organizer. Maximize the remaining space by sorting and stacking reusable containers by size.

021 EVALUATE YOUR POTS AND PANS

Pull out every single pot and pan—including woks, roasting pans, stockpots, and frying pans. Really think about each item and decide how often you use it. If it's pretty but you never use it, put it in the donate pile. If it's burnt, deeply scratched (in the case of nonstick pans), or made of aluminum, get rid of it. You only want healthy, high-quality pans in your home.

022 STORE POTS AND PANS CREATIVELY

Pots and pans can become the bane of your existence thanks to how difficult they are to keep organized. There are a few methods for storing them: hang them on a rail, slide them into multi-level wire racks, store them on an open shelf, or stack them in a cabinet. Depending on how much money you want to spend, you can even find some fancy systems at home improvement stores. For an inexpensive option, use vertical slotted file organizers (designed for office use) to store baking sheets, racks, and muffin pans.

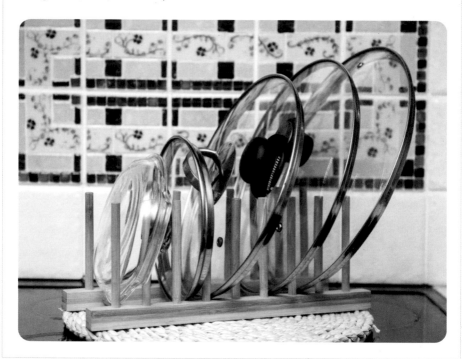

023 CONSIDER STORAGE

You might want to look at replacing an under-stove cabinet with deep slide-out drawers. Stack pans as tidily as possible, grouping like with like. Also consider a mounted pot rack or pegboard system, and designate a shallower drawer for storing the lids.

QUICK TIP

CHOOSE DISHWARE WISELY

If you're short on space, avoid splurging on over-the-top dishware. Instead, consider a versatile dish style in a neutral hue that can be dressed up or down depending on silverware, napkin rings, or other table dressings. You'll save a ton of cabinet space.

024 DOUBLE YOUR DISH STORAGE

Wire shelf racks will help you get the most out of your dish storage cabinet. You'll get twice the amount of surface area on each shelf, and you'll avoid a precarious, towering stack of plates or bowls. Stack dishware from largest to smallest to ensure a sturdy base.

025 HANG TEN

Mugs can be tricky. They're a pain to stack, and they take up a lot of valuable shelf space. Consider installing simple C-hooks underneath your upper cabinets for efficient hanging mug storage. (They're quite easy to screw in by hand.)

TOTE DISPOSABLES

Keep disposable or compostable dishware and utensils in a portable caddy or box. This allows for easy grab-and-go access if you're dining al fresco or doling out dessert at a party. Guests can help themselves to utensils as needed.

MAKE COUNTERTOPS A PAPER-FREE ZONE

Receipts, bills, catalogs, and other mail can build up easily on countertops, cluttering valuable surface area. The easiest way to prevent paper clutter is to avoid the dreaded "pile." Make a habit of sorting through papers as they come in to decide what should be filed and what can go straight to the recycling bin.

STORE INFREQUENTLY USED APPLIANCES

Be honest with yourself—how often are you really using that air fryer? How about your ice cream maker? Specialty appliances can be handy if you have the room to store them, but if you're short on kitchen space, move the ones you don't use on a weekly basis off the counter and into a cabinet or pantry.

028 HIDE SMALL BOTTLES

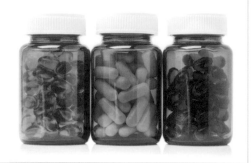

Pills, supplements, and vitamins that live outside the pantry don't need to sit out. Place frequently used bottles together in a basket or bin with a lid for handy access. See Item 071 for more information on how to properly and safely store medications.

029 EMBRACE A RETRO KITCHEN STAPLE

Bread boxes are not as in vogue as they once were, but consider adding a sleek, modern bread box or tin to your kitchen. It's handy for keeping bread, rolls, and buns tucked away.

QUICK TIP

DISPLAY MOST-USED DRY GOODS

If you keep frequently used dry ingredients on your counter (such as flour, sugar, coffee beans, or oats), consider investing in matching glass containers. While fancy containers aren't necessary for pantry containers, clear, uniform countertop storage will look and feel more organized.

030

KEEP COUNTERS LOOKING NEW

Counters are made from a wide variety of materials, so it can be tricky to be sure you're using the right cleaner. For example, white vinegar is a popular go-to cleaner, but it can't be used on stone countertops. The smartest and cheapest way to clean any type of countertop? Hot water, a little dish soap, and a microfiber cloth.

031 HANG IT UP

Removable wall hooks (like 3M Command hooks) will help you keep regularly used items off the counter. Hang up dish towels, washcloths, oven mitts, and more. Plus, dish towels will air out while they're hanging, so they won't acquire any musty odors.

CREATE PANTRY CATEGORIES

Keep track of dry goods in your pantry or cabinet by using categories. Think about how you cook: If you keep all your baking supplies together, it'll be obvious when you're running low on ingredients. The same applies for other categories, including canned goods, snacks, and spices. You can also categorize ingredients by cuisine. Make choices based on your cooking habits.

SPRUCE UP HARDWARE

Replacing hardware, such as handles and knobs, is an easy way to update cabinets, especially if your home is a rental. Replace rusty, outdated, or hard-to-use cabinet knobs to make your space feel new. When you move out, switch the old knobs back in and bring your new ones to your next place!

034 ADD COLOR TO CABINETS

If your kitchen feels dingy or outdated, repainting the cabinets might be a worthy investment. If you're a renter, your landlord might be more open to repainting than you might expect—they get an updated space, and you can make the kitchen feel like your own. Make sure you choose a paint finish that's easy to clean!

035 POP IN COLOR AND TEXTURE

Find fun ways to add personality and life to a neutral-colored kitchen. Try adding a stick-on faux-tile backsplash to your stove top area, or accessorize with functional accent pieces like a decorative tea kettle or cuckoo clock. Consider colorful vintage accessories.

036 EMBRACE ISLAND LIFE

Painting your kitchen island is one easy way to add color to an otherwise neutral-colored kitchen. It's easy to repaint if you get sick of the color, but it still makes a statement. If your kitchen doesn't have an island, invest in a rolling table or cart. It will give you another work surface and more storage, and you can wheel it out of the way when it's not in use.

037 EMBRACE MISMATCHED SEATING

Perfectly matching furniture is overrated. Mismatched furniture adds visual interest and gives you the option to switch out pieces one at a time without committing to a whole set. You can often find beautiful chairs on the cheap at estate or garage sales.

038 BRING NATURE INSIDE

Forage branches from outdoors and place them in a vase to create a beautiful (and free) decorative kitchen centerpiece. Their look and scent will move with the seasons, and you won't have to change them out as frequently as store-bought flowers.

039 GROW YOUR OWN HERBS

A light-filled kitchen windowsill is the perfect place for a miniature herb garden—it looks nice and serves a purpose. Many herbs will grow in water, so you don't need to worry about potentially messy soil. You can also regrow rooted veggie scraps in water, including scallions, romaine lettuce, and celery.

040
FIND SPACE ABOVE THE FRIDGE

The top of the refrigerator is an underutilized storage space—use it to stow away bins of extra glasses, paper goods, and extra pans. Bear in mind that it's not an ideal spot for food, as heat will escape from the top of the fridge and can cause things to spoil quickly.

041
GIVE YOUR FRIDGE A DEEP CLEAN

A clean kitchen just isn't complete without giving your refrigerator a good once-over. It's easy, takes less than an hour, and looks fabulous once you're done! Remove all drawers and shelves, scrub them clean with mild soap and water, and, when they are dry, apply a washable liner to each. It's stylish and, most importantly, absorbs spills. Replace the linings about every six months.

042
ORGANIZE REFRIGERATED GOODS

Use organizing bins on the shelves of your fridge. They're great for grouping like items such as condiments, preventing leftovers from getting lost in the back, and keeping kids' school lunches and snacks handy. You can also use containers inside the drawers to keep items like cheeses organized. When it's time to figure out what you need at the store, it only takes a quick glance to see what's needed for your shopping list.

043

DEEP CLEAN
YOUR FREEZER

Pull everything out of the freezer and dispose of anything expired or freezer-burnt. Donate anything that's still good but you know your family won't use. Take advantage of this time by cleaning the freezer inside and out.

044

CATEGORIZE YOUR
FREEZER ITEMS

Separate all your freezer items into categories based on how often you use them. Implement a colorful bin system to group your items. As a bonus, it will also make your freezer more eye-catching.

USE DRAWER DIVIDERS
AND BINS

Once you figure out how many categories you're dealing with, think about how to divide up the space. You can order bins or fancy freezer dividers online, or be a bit thriftier and make use of plastic reusable grocery bags. You will need at least one divider or container for each category.

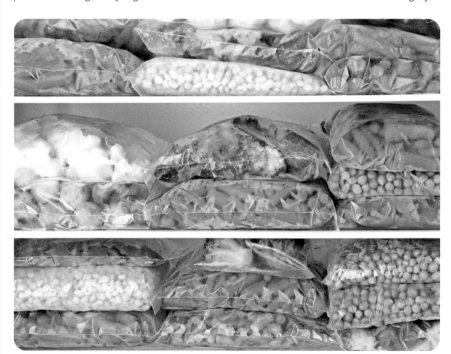

046

LABEL THE FRIDGE AND FREEZER

If you want to be even more organized, you can label each refrigerator and freezer section with a food category. It might seem too obvious, but it will help other family members put food away correctly after grocery shopping, and everyone will have an easier time finding what they need, which means less food waste in the long run.

047

SAY GOODBYE TO FREEZER BURN

Now that your freezer is ready and waiting, it's time to stock up on groceries and kiss freezer burn goodbye. Freezer burn isn't inevitable—you can prevent it if you use your newly organized freezer to your advantage. The bins will help prevent that frozen meat from languishing beneath a pile for weeks. Every month, sort through each bin so the oldest items get to be front and center. Go one step further and seal your food in freezer storage bags.

048

KEEP TRACK OF WHAT'S INSIDE

Don't let your freezer contents go unused. Use sticky notes or another labeling system to keep tabs on what's inside—without having to dive through the icy depths to find out. This will also help other meal planners and helpers know where to find the good stuff. (Unless, of course, you want to be the only one in charge of where the cheesecake is kept!)

049

LET
LIGHT IN

Light is important in the kitchen—being able to see what you're working on everywhere in the room opens up more workspace. Pendant lights are a great way to add pointed overhead lighting, and they're warmer than fluorescent overheads. If installing new lighting isn't in the budget, replace bulbs with a warmer light tone (soft white instead of cool white or daylight bulbs) to make the space feel more welcoming.

SAY GOODBYE TO LINOLEUM

Technology makes the look of wood accessible in a variety of materials like tile and vinyl. Vinyl is affordable, and tile is easy to clean; both are incredibly durable too.

QUICK TIP

STICK ON BACKSPLASH

Renters rejoice! There are more solutions than ever to hide dated kitchen backsplash in your apartment. Look for thin, peel-and-stick removable tile for an easy and affordable way to change the look of your space. And because the surface is tile, you can still wipe it down.

051 KEEP APPLIANCE PARTS TOGETHER

Never look for your food processor blade again! Make sure you store all appliance parts together, either inside the appliance itself or rubber-banded together and stowed nearby. A dedicated basket in your cabinet for spare appliance parts is another option.

052 BUY REUSABLE PRODUCTS

To clean green, you should really eliminate—or at least lighten your use of—paper towels. Invest in some microfiber cloths and keep them handy. You can also find reusable, environmentally friendly gloves to take care of your hands.

053 WASH YOUR DISHES THE GREEN WAY

For those with the option, it's more eco-friendly to wash your dishes in the dishwasher, since it uses less water than washing them by hand. If you don't have that option, soak your dishes first in hot, soapy water before hand-washing. This will loosen most tough food bits so you won't need the water running as you wash the dishes later on.

054

LOOK FOR NONTOXIC DISH DETERGENTS AND CLEANERS

Use natural brushes, silicone scrubbers, or a plant-based cleaning sponge to reduce microplastic pollution. Swap your regular dish soap for a nontoxic plant-based cleaning concentrate. Be sure to avoid synthetic dyes and fragrances, and choose phosphate-free soaps.

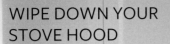

WIPE DOWN YOUR STOVE HOOD

A stove hood does a lot to keep a kitchen grime free. Make sure to return the favor by wiping it down regularly! You'll also want to make sure you clean the vent screens at least every two or three months.

056 ORGANIZE UNDER THE SINK

Space is at a premium under the kitchen sink, so make use of every bit of room to store your cleaning supplies.

CONSIDER THE SPACE Before you sort and clean, look at how the space is organized and how it can be more efficient. Consider stacking bins, trays, or 3M Command hooks for hanging.

SORT AND PURGE Throw away what you don't use, and sort remaining items by category (sponges and cloths, dish soap, household cleaners, etc.). If you discard anything toxic, consult your local waste management service to find out how to safely dispose of it.

PUT IT BACK Wipe down the area and organize your supplies into your chosen containers. Put everything back in an orderly fashion. If you're using Command hooks, note that they need to set for an hour before you hang anything on them.

THOROUGHLY CLEAN
THE KITCHEN SINK

It's good to clean the sink daily with an easy cleaner (see Item 013) and to follow it up with a weekly scrub. Follow these steps to a happier sink:

STEP ONE Rinse the dirty sink out really well, leaving no food particles or gunk.

STEP TWO Apply a cleaning paste like Shaklee Scour Off, using lots of elbow grease. Paste works better than most powdered cleaners, as it doesn't make big dust clouds and it adheres well to those vertical sink walls. If you don't have Scour Off, whip up a homemade cleansing paste using $^1/_2$ cup baking soda, a teaspoon of Castile soap, and just enough water to make a paste.

STEP THREE Scrub everything really well, then rinse off thoroughly.

STEP FOUR Spray the sink with a natural cleaning spray, then rinse again. Lastly, wipe down with a soft towel. Admire your handiwork and enjoy that sparkling sink!

058 KEEP YOUR SINK SCUFF-FREE

Pots and pans can leave marks in a white sink. To keep scuffing at bay, place wire sink grids with rubber feet at the bottom of the sink. Also, after cleaning your sink, try applying a thin coat of car wax (a tip from cleaning professionals). A wax-based stainless steel cleaner will help prevent fingerprints.

059 TAME THE JUNK DRAWER

What is a kitchen without a junk drawer? Its sole purpose is to contain items you have no designated spot for, so it's no wonder it gets out of hand in a hurry. Take a few minutes to go through your junk drawer and purge anything you haven't used in a while or anything that doesn't serve a purpose. You'll find that many items can be eliminated. Once you finish purging, remove the rest of the contents and wipe out the drawer. Then grab a few organizers (you can recycle cardboard jewelry boxes or sturdy plastic containers that you may have been saving) and categorize your miscellaneous items. Allow yourself a few minutes each month to go through the drawer and tidy it.

060 SHELVE OR HANG IT

Consider every possible place where you can add shelving for pantry essentials. If the containers are attractive enough, your essentials can be on display without feeling like clutter. Just don't let the shelves get messy or dusty. In addition, risers or additional shelves inside your cabinets are a great solution for smaller items, like canned goods, that can stack two or three levels deep. And racks that fit over cabinet doors are a great way to store spices, tea, and other small items. Hanging baskets can be used to hold fruit, garlic, and other items that would otherwise be taking up counter space.

061 SLIDE OUT

A lot of kitchens have cutting boards that slide out from under the counter and then stow away when no longer needed. If your kitchen doesn't have any, look into having them installed. It might be well worth it if you're working with very little counterspace.

062 FOLD DOWN

Many of us have heard tales of Depression-era relatives eating dinner off of fold-down ironing boards. The more workable version of this is a fold-out kitchen table. This addition can be a great option for adding a work surface or small dining space as needed.

063 WASTE NOT

One big challenge in a small kitchen is waste disposal, especially if you separate landfill trash, recycling, and compost. One great solution is a slide-out under-sink sorting system. You can find these bin systems at home improvement stores for under $100, and they're pretty easy to install. They usually consist of a metal rack and two to four sorting bins. You screw the metal rack into your under-sink cabinet, then mount the bins on the rack and you can then slide each bin in and out as needed. As a bonus, the system can keep pets or toddlers from monkeying with the trash.

064 UTILIZE YOUR VERTICAL SPACE

Hang pots and pans overhead, and consider mounting a sheet of pegboard for utensils. Install a small microwave on the wall or in a cabinet to free up counter space. Hanging mugs from hooks along the bottom of a shelf also frees up space and looks fun and cozy.

065 FIND ADDITIONAL STORAGE SPACE

Spots that are often used exclusively for decoration can actually become handy storage. The false-drawer front under most sinks can be replaced with a tilt-out tray that's great for storing sponges and scrub pads. Even more crafty, Ikea has a cupboard solution that sneaks a drawer into the bottom-of-the cabinet toe kick space. Attach small jars to the undersides of shelves and cabinets—you can just unscrew them when you need the spice or tea within, then screw them back on. Squeeze tall, skinny shelving units into any space you can. Even if the shelves that fit between your fridge and the wall can only hold a few cookbooks, those are cookbooks that aren't taking up space anywhere else! If there's space between your top cabinets and the ceiling, baskets and bins up there can hold rarely used items.

066 ORGANIZE YOUR PANTRY

Using a few containers, baskets, and bins, you can break down your pantry organization into categories and make the space work better for you. Start by categorizing the space and the items going into it. Chances are, you've got a lot of food taking up a lot of space. Use these groupings to sort out this magnet for madness: baking supplies (if you don't have a baking station), bulk items (rice, beans, and nuts), canned food, condiments, pasta and pasta sauces, chocolate and desserts, prepackaged food, and snacks.

067

CONTAIN WITH BASKETS AND COLOR-CODED PLASTIC BINS

Woven baskets are effective organizers for the pantry when you use them correctly. They're nice to look at, but the large sizes can become so full of food that you can't see what's at the bottom. However, baskets work well to store items like bags of food, snacks, prepackaged breakfast items, large quantities of the same item, and extra canned goods. Meanwhile, colorful bins are great for storing reusable food containers and their lids. You can use different colors to separate categories and make daily organizing a breeze.

068 BIN YOUR CANS

Organizing canned goods can be difficult to figure out. If you don't go through a huge amount of canned goods, they don't need to take up a lot of room in the pantry. Find some plastic storage bins of different sizes online and stack your cans in the bins horizontally.

069 CONTROL YOUR CANNED GOODS

Another option for corralling the various cans of soup, sauces, fruits, veggies, and other shelf-stable items is to utilize wall-mounted wire baskets—or an over-the-door organizer (see Item 073). These racks are often found in the closet storage sections of stores, rather than intended for pantry use, but some are perfectly sized for holding a rack of cans—and they're nice and sturdy, so they can support the heavy weight of all those cans.

070 START WITH AN INVENTORY

When you organize your pantry, keep track of what you have by using a pantry inventory sheet. You can keep your sheets on a physical clipboard, hanging a Command hook inside your pantry, or you can use an app or notepad on your phone. With your inventory tracked, grocery shopping will be a breeze.

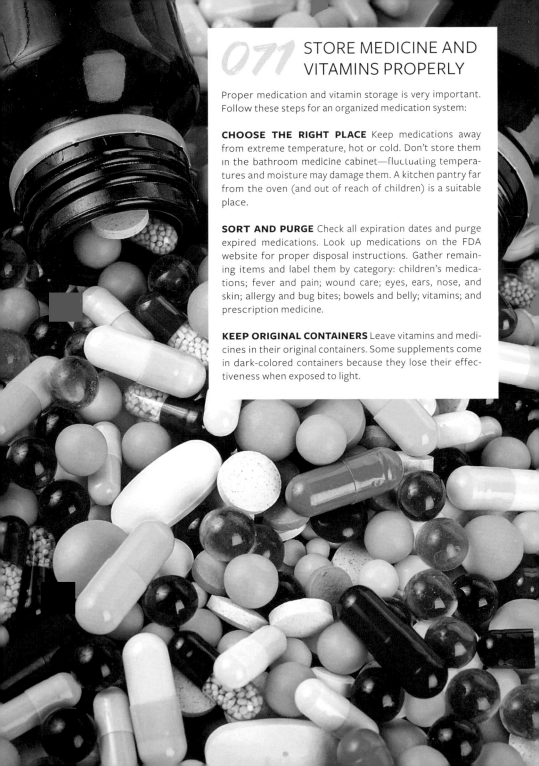

071 STORE MEDICINE AND VITAMINS PROPERLY

Proper medication and vitamin storage is very important. Follow these steps for an organized medication system:

CHOOSE THE RIGHT PLACE Keep medications away from extreme temperature, hot or cold. Don't store them in the bathroom medicine cabinet—fluctuating temperatures and moisture may damage them. A kitchen pantry far from the oven (and out of reach of children) is a suitable place.

SORT AND PURGE Check all expiration dates and purge expired medications. Look up medications on the FDA website for proper disposal instructions. Gather remaining items and label them by category: children's medications; fever and pain; wound care; eyes, ears, nose, and skin; allergy and bug bites; bowels and belly; vitamins; and prescription medicine.

KEEP ORIGINAL CONTAINERS Leave vitamins and medicines in their original containers. Some supplements come in dark-colored containers because they lose their effectiveness when exposed to light.

072

DESIGNATE A
GROWN-UPS CABINET

Many kitchens have at least one odd cabinet out, especially in rooms that aren't perfect squares or rectangles. These are good for storing medications and non-food substances you want the whole family to be aware—and careful—of. Teach your kids that this cabinet isn't for snacks and contains medicines and other grown-up items. Make sure it's part of an upper cabinet (out of very small children's reach) and that it's far enough from the oven to avoid heating up your meds (see Item 071). The whole family will know where to find the things that don't quite fit in with the rest of the kitchen.

073 USE YOUR DOORS

You don't want to forget to use the valuable space on the inside of your pantry doors. Door organizers can be found at most home stores or online. They work great for storing boxed food, sauces, and frequently used canned goods.

074 STORE FOOD IN CLEAR CONTAINERS

Clear containers, like the ones from OXO, are excellent for storing pasta, grains, and rice. When you get home from grocery shopping, empty the pasta boxes' contents into these containers. Cardboard food boxes clutter the space, so using clear containers helps you stay more organized.

075 HAVE FUN WITH LABELS

The neat text of a label maker might feel too cold or clinical for the pantry, but it's not your only option! Try using handwritten labels for a more personal feel. Or use chalk labels, which you can erase and reuse if the contents of the container change.

076 PLAN FOR SNACK ATTACKS

Set aside some time each week to portion out and pack up munchies. Use reusable containers to store and organize your snacks. Get all of the prep work done at one time. When washed and ready-to-go single servings are available, you'll save fruits and veggies from rotting in the fridge or on the counter before anyone remembers to eat them. Plus, when your appetite calls, you'll have a quick answer!

077

CREATE A SCHOOL-LUNCH STATION

Making school lunches can be a headache when all the components are scattered around the kitchen. Designate a drawer or shelf with enough room to store everything you'll need for assembly. Keep a small cutting board handy for sandwiches. Use smaller containers to separate items like snack and sandwich bags, utensils, tinfoil, Tupperware, and other components. Don't forget napkins and moist wipes. You can also save space by replacing hard lunch boxes with softer cloth bags (the insulated kinds are perfect) for more compact storage. Designating a special place for everything you need not only makes your morning routine run more smoothly—it also allows your children to help out.

078 SHOP
EFFECTIVELY

You might think a trip to the grocery store will be the same every time, but with an organized shopping list, it's faster and easier than ever before. If you have a regular weekly food shopping routine, step it up a notch by prepping your shopping list based on your kitchen inventory. Follow these steps for seamless shopping:

ALWAYS START WITH A MASTER LIST These are the items you need to replenish every week without fail. Store this on your phone or computer, print out several hard copies to keep in the kitchen, and add to it as needed.

MAKE SPACE Clear out the fridge and food storage areas to get rid of any too-old leftovers and make room for new purchases. Take stock of your pantry and decide what you need to buy.

HAVE A SEPARATE BULK LIST Keep a separate list for items you regularly buy in bulk, like paper products, bath products, snacks, pasta and rice, cooking oil, trash bags, batteries, storage products, frozen goods, and vitamins.

CONSULT YOUR LISTS Once you've got your master list, finalize it before you go to the store. Consult your weekly menu and add any new items you need. Check off items as you buy them. If there is a staple on the list that you don't need this week, cross it out.

079 UTILIZE YOUR FREEZER

For those of you on the go, especially if you have kids at home, your mantra should be, "Make the freezer your friend." Soups, side dishes, and desserts can easily be made in bulk and then stored in the freezer until you're ready to eat.

SOUPS Make stocks or soups up to two weeks in advance and store them in 2-cup (0.5-liter) portions for easy, single-serve defrosting.

BAKED GOODS Stock your freezer with muffins, pancakes, biscuits, scones, waffles, and other baked goods that can be frozen and toasted up later for a hot, buttery morning treat.

LEFTOVERS Double your recipes and store leftovers in individual packets so that you just have to throw them in the microwave for a quick, easy meal.

QUICK TIP

THAW OUT!

For easy reheating, transfer your frozen foods from the freezer to the refrigerator the night before, then bake in the oven. Add about 10 to 15 minutes if the center is still frozen.

080 DESIGN YOUR DINING AREA

The dining room is one of the spaces where we entertain our guests. It's also an area that shows our true personal style. Whether it's classic, contemporary, or vintage, choosing the right decor and pieces to fill the space will make it feel more authentic.

081 MAKE YOUR TABLE THE FOCAL POINT

The center of the space is the dining table. Make sure the table is the correct size to fit the room. If you have a small room, you will want a smaller table when you're not entertaining, but you can add a leaf in the middle to accommodate more guests for meals or buffets.

082

GET CREATIVE WITH YOUR CHAIRS

How many chairs do you have? Depending on the size of your family, at least six chairs at the table and two extras placed to the side should suffice. When you're not entertaining, you can put a chair on either side of the hutch. Chairs don't necessarily have to match the table. Think outside the box—you might like a white table and dark chairs, or mismatched antique chairs for an eclectic look.

CREATE A HOMEMADE COCKTAIL BAR

Shake up a fabulous martini by creating your very own cocktail bar. By investing in a few essential tools, spirits, mixers, and glasses, you'll be able to jazz up your night with dozens of cocktails at your fingertips. It's not necessary to stock your bar with every kind of liquor available. A bottle of each of the basics and a few mixers will do just fine. Don't want to purchase everything all at once? Begin with ingredients from your favorite drinks and go from there.

084 SHOWCASE YOUR COLLECTIBLES

Whatever it is that you collect, display it proudly in a cabinet or on a shelf. Place the same type of collectibles or décor near each other. Things display more beautifully as a collection than spread throughout your home. If your collectibles are breakable, make sure your cabinets have doors!

085

EMPLOY A DINING SIDEBOARD

When it comes to organizing the dining area, furniture that comes with a good amount of storage is key, especially if you like to entertain. Using a dining sideboard with shelving, drawers, and cabinets is the perfect way to contain this space, and you can find pieces of furniture in many styles and sizes. Store your seasonal table décor, holiday dishes, and serving trays and bowls in your cabinets. Display your china, cake stands, pictures frames or other décor, and vintage dishes on the shelves. Fill the drawers with napkin rings, cloth napkins, place mats, chargers, tablecloths and runners, extra silverware, place cards, and candles and lighters.

QUICK TIP

STAY FOCUSED

Keep your sideboard exclusively for dining and entertainment storage. Remove all other items that belong elsewhere.

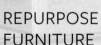

REPURPOSE FURNITURE

If you don't have a sideboard, you get to be creative! You might want to reuse a piece of furniture you already own, giving it a fresh coat of paint and a new life in your efficient, organized dining area. Line the drawers and insert bins and organizers to hold necessities for mealtime or entertaining.

087 ADD A BUFFET

If you entertain a lot, add a buffet to your dining area. This is where you place food for dinner parties or holiday celebrations. You can also use it to store liquor, wine, and cocktail glasses.

088 USE BINS FOR HIDE-AND-SEEK

Open shelving on the bottom of a buffet or sideboard isn't the best spot to keep dishes, especially if you have pets or small children. Place bins or baskets in your sideboard—they'll allow you to use this storage space without risking broken dishware. Use them to store cloth napkins, candlesticks, extra silverware, platters, and other less frequently used dinnerware.

089 CIRCLE UP

If you're short on space, you can still create a dedicate dining area. A round table usually seats more people than a rectangular one, has a smaller footprint, and can be easily moved into a corner to make more floor space when needed.

090 DOUBLE UP

It's okay to double-dip on how a space is used. A nice bar or counter can also be a cute diner-style eating surface for two. One hint: choose your barstools well. Without a footrest, you might end up feeling as if your legs are asleep halfway through dinner.

091 KNOW WHEN TO FOLD 'EM

Some folding tables are surprisingly chic, so don't discount this option without shopping around a bit. You can also look into tables that fold down from the wall, Murphy bed–style. You can also install a slide-out table under a counter, which you can eat on or use as an extra serving surface at parties.

092 TURN OVER A LEAF

Tables with insertable leaves can be a great option if you have guests over a lot—just be sure you have a good spot to stash the leaves when they're not in use. Drop-leaf tables are another option, offering up extra dining space in a jiffy.

093 GET A LEG UP

If you have a space to store the pieces when not in use, a tabletop with screw-in legs can assemble easily, and the end result can be quite stylish.

094 WORK WITH YOUR LIGHTING

To help define a small dining space, lighting can make a huge difference. Try hanging a pendant lamp over the table—especially if the table's not in a designated dining room. This really helps set the space apart from the rest of the room. If you rent your home or can't hang a light for other reasons, a nice lamp placed high behind the table is an alternate solution.

095 DEFINE THE SPACE

Another way to create a space within a space is to hang something on the wall that draws the eye upward and visually anchors the table. It might be a big mirror, a framed piece of art, or a funky wall clock. Experiment with what works in your home.

096

FOR ICE, EMPLOY THE KITCHEN (OR BATHROOM)

When entertaining, storing ice and cold drinks can be tricky. Rather than filling a bucket with ice and dragging it to your dining area, fill up the sink (or bathtub) with ice and drinks. They'll be out of your way, and once they're cold, you can bring them out to your guests. If you're hosting an outdoor shindig, see Item 099.

097

KEEP A GARBAGE CAN HANDY

Most people don't keep trash or recycling cans in their dining area, but if you entertain often, it can be a wise option. Your guests will be able to throw their own garbage away without wandering into your kitchen, which will help ease the flow of foot traffic, keep serving surfaces clear, and cut down on your cleanup time.

098

BE READY TO PARTY

It's always a good idea to keep party supplies on hand for impromptu celebrations. Label a large shoebox "Party Box" and fill it with the necessities. The box should include candles, balloons, streamers, cake decorating items, and any festive banners you might want to pin up. Candles are easy to misplace, so having these in a dedicated spot means you don't need to purchase them over and over. When stocking your party supply box, remember to shop sales and clearance sections after the holidays. Prices for party supplies hit rock bottom during these times.

099

KEEP DRINKS COOL IN THE POOL

When entertaining outdoors, ditch the tiny cooler and pile drinks and ice into a kiddie pool—a festive touch for a backyard BBQ. Kiddie pools are very affordable, and they provide plenty of space to hold drinks for everyone. Plus, you'll keep your guests from constantly going inside to your fridge.

QUICK TIP

EAT OUTSIDE!

In the summer, one fun idea is to take advantage of the weather and eat meals outdoors. A picnic in the backyard is a great way to get some sun and avoid a lot of the meal cleanup you'd otherwise be doing. If you have a backyard grill or firepit, you can roast hot dogs or make s'mores as a special treat. They're even more fun in the afternoon at home, because it's unexpected!

100 STORE OUTDOOR UTENSILS

Disposable paper products and plastic cutlery are often used for cookouts, birthday parties, or times when you just can't wash another dish. Designate a cabinet or basket in your kitchen to store these items for easy use and cleanup. To avoid being wasteful, consider purchasing reusable melamine dishes in place of the disposable ones, or purchase compostable paper and plastic products so you're not adding to the landfill. These are made from recycled, biodegradable materials, and you can find plates, cups, utensils—you name it. Another option is to buy a cheap set of "real" utensils and keep them with the outdoor supplies. Include the following with your outdoor entertaining items: plates, bowls, cutlery, napkins, cups, tablecloths, straws, cupcake cups (for snacks), and toothpicks (for finger foods).

101 SET THE TONE FOR YOUR HOME

The foyer is the first space you see each time you enter your home. It should greet you—and others—with open arms. Because this space sets the tone for your home, it should be clean, welcoming, and clutter-free at all times. It should also reflect your taste and the general aesthetic of your household. After all, you never know when your next guest will drop in.

102 ESTABLISH A CLEAN SLATE

The first and most important step is to deep clean the space. Empty it completely and scrub it down from top (including the crown molding and light fixtures) to bottom (the floors, including grout, if you have a tiled entryway). Make the whole place shine! Wipe down the front door (inside and outside), all moldings, baseboards, chair rails, doorknobs, locks, mirrors, and walls. If there's a staircase, clean it up, dust the rails and surfaces, and wash any rugs or curtains. Declutter the hall closet if you've got one. A clean foyer is the number one priority when setting the tone for your home.

103 CHOOSE THE RIGHT FURNITURE

Entryways come in all shapes and sizes, so really thinking about your space and your needs will help inform wise purchases. If you're short on square footage, a slim console table with storage is ideal (see Item 118). If you have a small space but high ceilings, consider a tall vertical cabinet that can go flush against the wall.

104 FAKE YOUR BUILT-INS

Cubby-style built-in shelving is having a design moment, and you can get the same look without paying for a custom job. Mimic the appearance of built-ins by installing multiple separate cubby units in your entryway—it'll look as if a pro did them, and you'll be free to rearrange them as your storage needs change.

105 GET HOOKED

If you can't fit a full table in your entryway, install wall hooks instead—they're a great way to store coats, hats, and even bags and backpacks. Although it's important to love the looks and finish of your hooks, make sure they're substantial enough to hold weight and a good shape so that things aren't constantly slipping off.

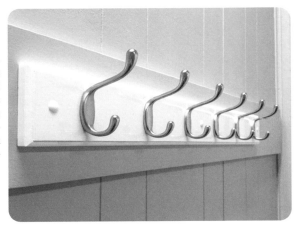

106 CREATE A CATCH-ALL

The best way to prevent paper clutter is to stop it where it starts, so invest in a basket, hanging bin, or tray in your entryway for mail. When mail comes in, look through it immediately to see what needs your attention. Then recycle the rest. If you have space, add a small bin or basket for junk mail that you can take out with the rest of your recyclables.

107 FILE ON THE WALLS

Take a cue from the office and look for an upscale, home-friendly version of a wall-mounted file organizer. This is a great option if you don't have room for baskets or bins in your entryway. Fabric wall organizers are perfect for sorting mail, and you can also use them for pet essentials like leashes and baggies.

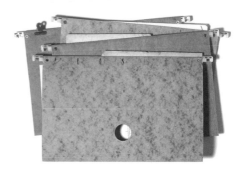

108 ASSIGN DESIGNATED SPOTS

Find a few boxes or baskets for all your foyer items, like handbags, shoes, wallets, scarves, hats, umbrellas, sports gear, school bags, books, keys, and mail (see Item 106). Don't let the tabletop become a catchall space for items people drop on their way in the door—the table will become buried almost instantly, you'll never be able to find the item you need, and your organized entryway will go out the window. Label each container for categories such as winter wear, rain gear, shopping bags, pets.

109 CORRAL COATS AND SHOES

Keep the hall closet free from clutter as much as possible. Designate the space for coats, shoes, and bags only—or implement a system that works for your family. You can also keep a basket and a coat hook near your front door for these items. Another handy way to use your space efficiently is to hang a shoe organizer rack on the inside of the closet door. This will keep shoes off the floor and out of the way. If you don't mind the shoes but want to avoid the dirt, put down a textured mat for feet-wiping, or a pebbled boot tray to drain water—you can DIY one with some river stones for an attractive, no-puddles solution for rainy days.

110 CATCH DIRT IN THE RUG

This is the easiest way to cut down on cleaning time. Invest in a rug for your entryway to catch dirt as it comes in, so it won't get tracked all over the house. When choosing a rug, stay away from anything too delicate—this item will get a lot of use and will show shabbiness sooner than other parts of the space. Materials like sisal and jute are very durable, and wool is both durable and naturally stain resistant. If you're especially tough on rugs, look for an indoor/outdoor version instead. An entryway rug works hard, so it should be replaced or deep cleaned every year.

111 CREATE A FAUX FOYER

Some living spaces just don't lend themselves to a traditional foyer, particularly small homes or railroad-style apartments with long hallways and small rooms. In these homes, your best bet might be to break up your foyer into multiple pieces around your house, with each function handled at its own station. Think about how you move through the space when you enter your home and set up stations accordingly.

112 AVOID THE MORNING RUSH

Designating a place in your entryway for essentials like keys, wallets, phones, and purses will help minimize frantic searches on busy mornings. Place a key rack or hooks on the inside of the door, or use a small tray on your entryway table. Make a practice of placing critical small items there when you get home so they're always at hand when you head out in the morning.

113 MAKE SEASONAL SWAPS

Let yourself off the (literal) hook and let go of the idea that every piece of outerwear must stay in your entryway year round. Instead, get used to doing a seasonal swap to avoid crowding. You'll thank yourself later when you're not digging through winter mittens in search of your favorite summer scarf.

114 MAKE THE CLOSET WORK HARDER

If you have a small coat closet in your entryway, find ways to make the most of what you have. Look for closet rod extenders and hanging canvas organizers to multiply the amount of storage space. Place baskets or bins at the bottom of the closet to turn the floor into usable organizational space.

115 TRY FLOATING SHELVES

This is one way to add decorative elements to your entryway without losing functional surface area. Floating shelves are a breeze to install (and relatively renter friendly) and can be used to display art, plants, and photographs.

116 CREATE A MUDROOM

If your indoor space is limited but you do have a garage, consider setting up a mudroom area there. Maximizing how you use this space is key, especially if you have school-age kids (since they come with lots of shoes, coats, book bags, and such). This mudroom takes less than an hour to put together and works like a charm.

YOU'LL NEED

- 2 pieces pine board (measure your space to determine what size you need)
- Nail gun or hammer and nails
- 3M Command wood stabilizer strips (or other variety)
- Decorative trim
- Paint and paintbrush
- Scotch extreme fasteners
- 3M Command hooks
- Name tags

STEP ONE Measure the space and determine what lengths of wood you'll need, how many hooks, and so forth. Gather all your supplies and tools and be sure everything is within easy reach.

STEP TWO Fasten the pieces of wood together using your nail gun or hammer, then tack on the stabilizer strips. Add decorative trim to the top of your panel.

STEP THREE Paint the wood panel and let it dry.

STEP FOUR Hang your panel on the wall with the fasteners, or nail it to wall studs. Then apply the Command hooks to the panel or screw in hooks of your choosing.

STEP FIVE Label the hooks with each family member's name and hang up those jackets and accessories! Remember that the hooks need an hour to cure before you can hang anything on them.

ADD VERTICAL STORAGE, BASKETS, AND BOOT TRAYS

Wherever your mudroom space is located, it's important to stay organized. Wall-mounted baskets are great for shopping bags, umbrellas, and other frequently used items. You can also use one as a spot for outgoing mail. A shelf with high-up bins can hold seasonal outerwear for when it's needed. A nice basket can hold spare kids' shoes and rain items. It's also essential to have a boot tray to keep those wet wellies from making a mess.

118 MAKE YOUR CONSOLE TABLE A STAR

Console tables offer extra storage to fit shoes or even a low wire basket underneath. If you chose a console table with added storage space, look for one with solid doors, so you can add 3M Command hooks on the inside.

119 STASH OLD TOWELS

You might be tempted to toss old towels, but if you have kids or pets, they might just be your new best friend. Keep old towels in a bin with a lid, and when wet weather comes, grab one to dry off wet boots, belongings, or a muddy-pawed pet. It will save you time cleaning rugs, tiles, and even the walls.

120 CREATE AN OPTICAL ILLUSION

Paint can be a clever way to make a room feel larger. If your home's entryway is more like a hallway, painting the area can create a sense of separate space. If painting isn't an option, consider using peel-and-stick wallpaper.

121 WORK WITH YOUR RADIATOR

Perhaps you have a wall where a console table could fit perfectly, but an old-fashioned radiator is sitting in the way. Make it work by buying or building a radiator cover that's designed to release heat. Now you're got a surface that works for you, instead of a radiator that works against you.

122 EMPOWER KIDS

Make it easy for your kids to help keep the entryway organized by making their most-used items accessible. Ensure coat hooks and bins that hold jackets and outdoor gear are low enough for kids to reach. Keep your organizing system simple enough for them to understand so they can put things away on their own. For young kids, use stickers with pictures to label storage containers.

123 INSTATE A SHOE POLICY

Though the occasional entryway pileup is inevitable, make a rule that shoes need to go back to their regular homes once a week. Make sure shoes have a regular home in a closet or the garage. Letting shoes dry on a boot tray in an entryway is perfectly acceptable, but don't let them languish there. When you keep shoes out of the pile, they stay cleaner and in better shape.

124 GET IN THE ZONE

No matter how large or small a room is, looking at it as a collection of zones is a great way to manage clutter and maximize the room's functionality. This is true of every room in the house, but because the living room is used for so many purposes, the zone system is perhaps most important and effective here. Before you even start thinking about how to divide up the space, give it a thorough cleaning. Get rid of anything you don't like or use, remove items that belong in other rooms, take out the trash, and in any other way you can, simplify the space.

125 LOVE YOUR LAYOUT

Think about traffic flow in the room and how it's most used. Can you put your office space in an alcove or corner where you can tune out the rest of the room and really focus? If you entertain frequently, be sure that sofas and chairs are grouped well for conversation. If your living room is long and narrow, visually divide it into two conversation zones by using a rug in one space and grouping furnishings accordingly.

126 DON'T PUSH IT ALL AGAINST THE WALL

In a small space, it might feel tempting to push all your furniture against the walls. Counterintuitively, this can make a room feel smaller. Instead, set up furniture in zones geared toward activities such as watching TV, reading, or chatting with guests.

127 CREATE THE PERFECT READING SPOT

If your family loves to read, set up a reading corner in the room. Place a comfortable chair and a lamp in the space, with a bookshelf nearby. Display books on the shelf, organized by genre, with the children's books at the bottom for easy reach. Place a basket by the chair to collect newspapers and magazines for recycling. You can also consider adding a built-in window seat to an otherwise underutilized wall. For a storybook feel, frame a window with bookshelves on either side and a seat in between.

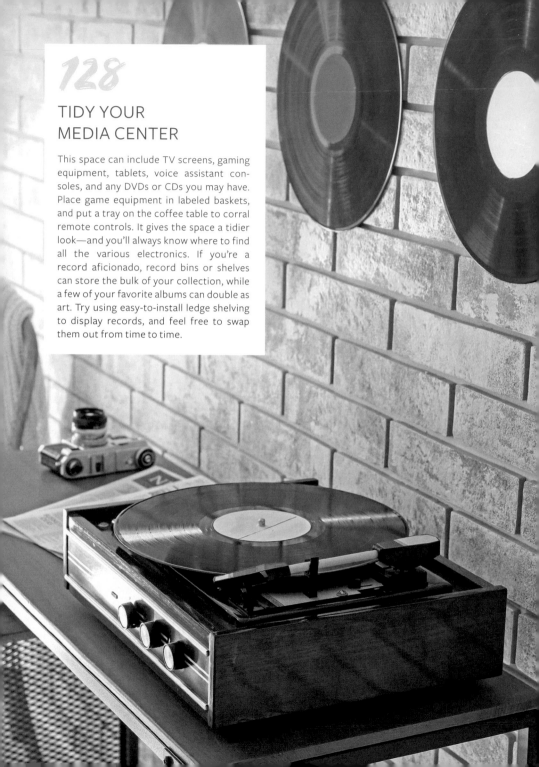

128

TIDY YOUR MEDIA CENTER

This space can include TV screens, gaming equipment, tablets, voice assistant consoles, and any DVDs or CDs you may have. Place game equipment in labeled baskets, and put a tray on the coffee table to corral remote controls. It gives the space a tidier look—and you'll always know where to find all the various electronics. If you're a record aficionado, record bins or shelves can store the bulk of your collection, while a few of your favorite albums can double as art. Try using easy-to-install ledge shelving to display records, and feel free to swap them out from time to time.

129 CHERISH YOUR MEMORIES

Store photo albums and keepsakes neatly together on bookshelves. Consider replacing old or mismatched photo albums.

130 MAKE SPACE FOR YOUR HOBBIES

Board games, toys, playing cards, knitting projects, and the like can be stored in storage ottomans or shelf-friendly baskets. Storing things out of sight keeps the space looking clutter-free.

131 STRATEGICALLY ARRANGE YOUR FURNITURE

Where you place your furniture will depend on how your family uses it. If your family loves watching movies and shows, the TV (or projector screen) will be the focus of your living room. Move the sofa and chairs to face the screen, but make sure their occupants can still converse. If your family plays a lot of card or board games around the coffee table, you'll want to cluster chairs or floor cushions nearby. And if you're a family of conversationalists, move the couch and chairs to face each other. To streamline the space, store extra blankets or pillows out of sight.

132 DUST AND VACUUM REGULARLY

Your living room is a hardworking space, so keep it clean! When dusting, start with the highest surfaces and work your way down to prevent dust from drifting onto already clean surfaces. Vacuum your living room once a week—consider investing in a lightweight stick vacuum to make quick cleanups easy. When vacuuming carpets, move in alternating directions, vertically, and then horizontally to lift more dirt and dust. During your seasonal deep clean, move furniture, vacuum the cushions, and use the detailing attachment to suck up dust along the baseboards.

133 MAKE CLEANUP EASIER

If you have pets or small kids, sofa slipcovers and pillow covers are a blessing. It's easy to toss covers into the washing machine with a detergent booster to get them clean. Wash them seasonally to help prevent permanent stains.

134 DON'T FORGET ABOUT THE CURTAINS

Pet hair can do a real number on curtains. Washing them once a season, or at least twice a year, will keep them looking presentable. It also works better than the vacuum's upholstery attachment.

135 THINK ABOUT PAINT

When considering painting, think about your room as a whole. If you have plenty of color in your furniture and accessories, go for a white paint or another neutral hue. Use a bolder color to balance out neutral-colored accessories. If your home has trim, paint it all one color to unify the space. No matter what, be sure to pick up swatches or test paint colors on the wall before you commit.

136 BE MINDFUL OF BUILT-INS

Don't let built-ins collect clutter. Built-ins should be curated just like any other shelf, especially if they're open or have glass doors. Grouping glassware by color or type can create an orderly, attractive look. If you have a dark cabinet, go for a contrasting look by filling it with light or white pieces.

137
REORGANIZE YOUR BOOKSHELF

Gather all of the books in your home and place them in one central location. Sort through each book, categorizing as suits your storage scheme (perhaps by genre or size) and purging those you no longer need. Consider only keeping the books that you will read or refer back to later. Once you've sorted through, replace the keepers on your bookshelf.

138
DISTRIBUTE COLORS EVENLY

It might be tempting to color-block your books, but distributing colors evenly throughout a bookshelf will help it feel more visually balanced. For variety, try stacking your books in alternating horizontal and vertical arrangements. In empty spots on shelves, display art and other keepsakes.

139
GET ONE, REMOVE ONE

In the future, when you plan to purchase a new book, use the "one in, one out" rule. If you purchase one, donate one. This eliminates clutter and alleviates storage issues.

140 STORE YOUR DVDS

If you have a DVD collection, get rid of cases and transfer the discs to a binder or CD wallet that can be easily tucked away on a shelf. Look for a version with transparent pockets and alphabetize your discs so you don't have to search through your whole movie collection every time you want to watch one.

141 PUT IT BACK

Conquer the clutter that builds up in the living room by establishing a family rule to always put things away. Have your kids put their toys away in their designated spots before they go to sleep. Similarly, if you're knitting while watching a show, don't just put the project down and walk away. Store your supplies somewhere tidy but close at hand, like in a basket on a nearby shelf.

142 GROUP LIKE WITH LIKE

Stash essential items so that you can lay your hands on them easily—without having to lay your eyes on them all the time. Group similar items into categories (remotes, magazines, blankets, neck or back pillows) and store them together in a basket, bin, tray, or caddy.

143 CLIMB THE WALLS

If your living room lacks shelves, consider hanging baskets on the walls to hold magazines, charging cords, or other items. If your living room is by your entryway, mount a basket for mittens, hats, and scarves right by the door, so they're there when you need them rather than scattered around the house.

144 TAKE A MOMENT

Whenever you walk into or out of your living room, take a moment to notice if anything's out of place and if it's easy to fix, just do it right then and there while you're thinking about it. That means folding the blanket and stashing it in a bin, reshelving books, taking your teacup back to the kitchen, and otherwise keeping chaos at bay, one step at a time.

145 SHOW OFF BLANKETS

Instead of hiding blankets in a storage basket, consider hanging them from decorative hooks or a slim vintage ladder leaned against the wall. Many throw blankets have beautiful detailed patterns, and can add color and texture to your room. This option also saves floor space and allows blankets to air out, preventing mildew.

146

MAKE FURNITURE DO DOUBLE DUTY

It seems as if furniture designers have finally realized that people have a lot of stuff—and that they need somewhere to put it! If storage is limited in your house or if you find yourself with a lot of items that you use frequently enough that it would be silly to stash them in the basement or attic, you might be able to hide them in plain sight.

147

USE A BENCHWARMER

Padded benches are often suggested as a versatile furnishing choice for smaller rooms, as they take up less space than a couch or love seat. Many benches also do double duty as storage spots, either under a lift-up seat like a traditional piano bench, or behind a chic skirt. Some modern versions simply put the bench on top of shelves or cubicles, so you can display books or keepsakes low to the ground.

148 HIDE IT
IN THE SOFA

Cleverly constructed couches offer under-arm consoles for all of those things you don't want to get up and go fetch once you're comfy, while other sofas sit on top of slide-out drawers or have under-cushion compartments. If you have a pull-out couch for guests, stash clean linens (in fabric bags) between the cushions. Then you'll have everything ready if you need to make up a bed for the evening.

149 GET HELP FROM SHELVES

Sometimes it doesn't take much to make a big difference in a piece of furniture's utility. A coffee table with cubbies underneath it, or an end table with a shelf or two near the ground, can help contain items that get scattered or look messy.

150 MULTITASK WITH OTTOMANS

The humble footstool can be a multitasking superhero. There are many models that include storage space in addition to their footrest capabilities—from cubes that open up to stash lots of goodies to more elegant pieces with hidden compartments. And when you suddenly have more guests than chairs, an ottoman makes a great casual seat.

151 BUILD IN STORAGE

If you're lucky, your home came with built-in storage in every corner—but if not, you can add built-in fixtures through means as simple as a bookshelf and some crown molding. For example, if you have a ton of books and no library to store them in, built-in bookshelves can transform a room. Consider slender, floor-to-ceiling shelves with a relatively shallow depth: The minimal footprint preserves floor space and opens up vertical storage for books, media, keepsakes, and baskets that would otherwise take up valuable surface area.

152 MULTITASK FURNISHINGS

Get creative with how you use furniture. Storage ottomans help you stash things out of sight and also serve as additional seating for casual gatherings (see Item 150). Use a funky chest instead of a table in order to store extra textiles, or look into coffee tables that lift up to become a dining or work table if needed. If you have overnight guests often, consider a stylish futon (they do exist) or pullout sofa bed.

153 MINIMIZE ELECTRONICS

A wall-mounted flat-screen TV saves space, and a good laptop can easily replace a bigger desktop computer. Use your phone or tablet to stream music to Bluetooth speakers and you won't have to find space for a bulky stereo.

154 HIDE TECH WHERE YOU CAN

Hide your cable box and internet router in a decorative box, and then surround the box with books and other knickknacks. Thread power cords along the backsides of bookshelves instead of letting them hang down. Alternatively, tuck electronics away in a cabinet or closet.

155 SHOW SOME LEG

The more floor space is visible, the bigger a space seems. Choose chairs, tables, and sofas with legs that elevate them above the ground and avoid old-fashioned skirted designs. Nesting tables with slender legs are a versatile way to save space and expand surfaces when needed. Choose tall floor lamps to avoid using precious table space, or go for wall sconces for the ultimate in space-saving economy.

156 MIX IT UP

If you're in a small space, you might be tempted to keep everything small, but one big accent piece can really give a room character. It could be a big piece of art or an oversized chair. Look for furniture with an eye to versatility. An armoire might make a cool desk, with kids' toys stored in the drawers.

 ## GET
CLEAR

Glass-topped tables vanish into the room and help things feel less crowded. For a retro look, check out clear acrylic end tables. A couple of cubes can make a small coffee table, double as storage, and be easily stashed away.

 ## USE A COFFEE TABLE
FOR BALANCE

Get creative with the shape of your coffee table. A round or oval table might look right at home in a room with a lot of rectangular, boxy furniture. For maximum versatility, an ottoman with a tray can double as a coffee table.

159 EDIT THE TABLETOP

Be intentional about what you keep on your coffee table—it should reflect you and your interests. Include a variety of objects in different shapes and sizes: something tall and thin, like a vase with branches or strawflowers; something low and horizontal, like books or a decorative storage box; and other conversation-starting items like a candle, geode, or other accent piece. Avoid clutter, though—remember to leave some space to use the table as a table!

160 CONSIDER A COFFEE-TABLE TRAY

Place aesthetically pleasing decorative pieces on a tray. Then when you need to use the table more functionally, it'll be easy to move the tray or slide it underneath the table.

161 MAKE YOUR BOOKSHELVES POP

Say no to monotone! Add some interest to your shelves by painting the interior surfaces a different color from the exterior (or adding patterned wallpaper). This will draw attention to the items on the shelves and add a nice hit of color to a room.

162

HIDE STORAGE IN PLAIN SIGHT

When looking into storage solutions, choose pieces that fit in with the architecture of the room. Painting them the same color as the rest of the room makes them even more subtle, offering sneaky extra storage without visual crowding.

163 CHOOSE SCONCES

If you have a corner with a small table but not enough room for a lamp, add a sconce to the wall. They're easy to install, and they allow you to keep surfaces clear. If you are a renter, look for models with easy plug-in cords so you don't have to hardwire them into the wall.

164 HANG PLANTS FROM ABOVE

Keep surfaces clear by mounting hooks on the ceiling (or a wall grid) for hanging plants. This is also a great way to prevent energetic kids and pets from knocking over your favorite pothos plant.

165 HIDE BEHIND THE COUCH

If your couch is located centrally in the room, consider placing a slim profile table or shelf behind it for subtle storage. This is a great place to store books, toys, games, and all of those things you need when you're lounging on the couch.

166 MAKE CURTAIN HEIGHT COUNT

Here's a clever way to make your living room feel larger: Hang curtain rods higher than the window frames, placing them as close as you can to the ceiling without taking away from their function. This trick draws the eye upward, making your ceilings feel higher.

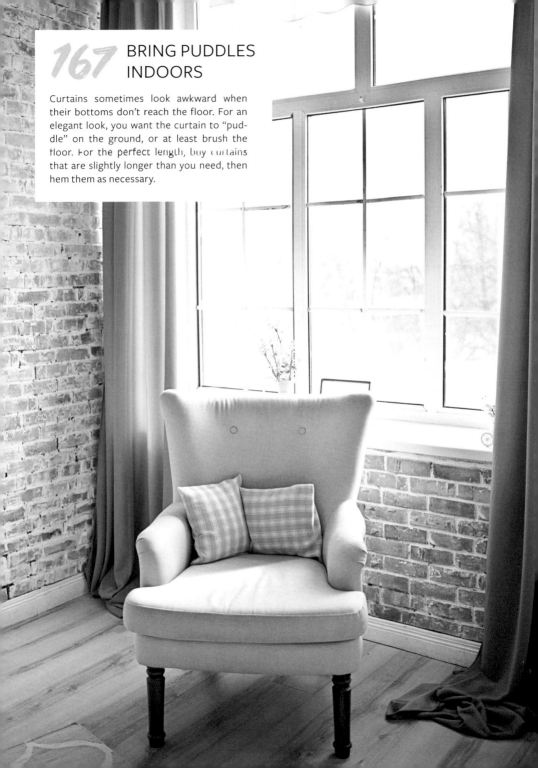

167 BRING PUDDLES INDOORS

Curtains sometimes look awkward when their bottoms don't reach the floor. For an elegant look, you want the curtain to "puddle" on the ground, or at least brush the floor. For the perfect length, buy curtains that are slightly longer than you need, then hem them as necessary.

168 REFRESH YOUR BEDROOM

The main bedroom should be a sanctuary: a place for relaxation, not stress. If yours is bursting with clothes, extra linens, work papers, kids' toys, and other nonessential items, you are likely in dire need of a refresh. Luckily, it won't take more than an afternoon of your time. Work in one area at a time, clearing out anything that doesn't belong in a bedroom, donating anything you no longer need or use, and storing anything that needs to be properly corralled. Remember that less is more, and be methodical. Reading chairs, ottoman benches, and door hangers can become magnets for clothes and bags that didn't make it to their proper places. Move the stray items to their proper homes and watch your bedroom become your domain of peace and calm once more.

169 TAKE ADVANTAGE

There will never be a better time to deep clean your bedroom. Clean all those spots that go neglected—the windows, doorknobs, moldings, and baseboards—and then vacuum and dust. Wash the bed linens, curtains, and bed skirt.

170 PUT IT ALL AWAY

Once you've cleaned your space, make sure you keep the organization a habit and don't let the clutter overcome you! Clutter creates anxiety, which is the opposite of peacefulness. By simply cleaning up after yourself, you will remove the negativity associated with the mess.

171 WASH LINENS WEEKLY

It takes time and effort, but if you make it a habit to wash your bedding every week, you will slip into those sheets each night with a feeling of calmness and relaxation.

172 MAKE A DIY LINEN SPRAY

Use this linen spray to usher all your senses into a restful state. Feel free to use your essential oil of choice.

YOU'LL NEED
- 1 tablespoon isopropyl alcohol
- 20 drops lavender essential oil
- Filled bottle of distilled water

In a 4-oz (0.1-liter) spray bottle, combine all ingredients. Blend together by shaking the bottle, and shake well before each use. Spray lightly onto pillows and sheets before you get into bed for a restful night's sleep.

173 USE THE SPACE UNDER YOUR BED

If you live in a small home or you're lacking essential storage or closet space in your bedroom, you can implement under-bed storage. Many beds come with built-in drawers, but you can modify your existing bed too. Add casters to the bottoms of wooden boxes to create rolling drawers that fit neatly beneath the bed skirt, or purchase flat plastic bins for storing shoes, out-of-season clothes, sheets, and blankets. If your bed doesn't allow for storage underneath, consider getting bed risers or investing in a bed frame with under-bed storage. It frees up space for little-used items like suitcases or memorabilia.

174 ADD END-OF-BED STORAGE

A storage bench at the foot of your bed is a convenient place to store extra blankets or out-of-season items like coats and sweaters. Plus it provides a great place to set out an outfit for the next day or to sit while you put your shoes on in the morning,

175
THE MULTIPURPOSE OTTOMAN STRIKES AGAIN

Storage ottomans can be used in the bedroom too—place one at the foot of the bed to store extra bedding, and it will become a functional part of your bedroom. Some are even specially designed for shoe storage, with dividers or pockets to hold pairs of dress shoes or sneakers.

176 MAKE ROOM FOR DOGS

Have a dog that sleeps in your room? Instead of a bulky dog bed or carrier, get a cushion or crate that blends in with the décor. Nowadays there are versions that look like regular tables or nightstands, with a flat top and a crate underneath. It gives Fido a place of his own without sacrificing on surface area.

177 GET CORDS OFF THE FLOOR

Some power strips come with holes in them, making it easy to attach them to the wall. Consider mounting your power strip on the wall behind your nightstand to keep it out of sight but still close enough to charge any electronics you want to keep nearby.

178 USE THE PERFECT PILLOW FORMULA

There is such a thing as too many pillows—if you overdo it, they're a pain to store and you'll be moving them on and off the bed constantly. Here's a can't-fail formula: two regular pillows with pillowcases, two regular pillows with shams, two European-sized pillows, and a lumbar pillow. This offers just enough volume without overwhelming your bed.

179 LAYER IN TEXTURED BEDDING

The secret to that catalog bed look is volume, and you can achieve that by layering your bedding. In addition to sheets and a (thin) quilt, add a fluffy duvet and finish it off with a chunky knit throw at the end of the bed. At bedtime, use what you need and remove what you don't.

180 UTILIZE NIGHTSTANDS WITH DRAWERS

Nightstands without drawers are an invitation for clutter. Nightstand drawers offer you a place to stash bedside essentials like reading glasses, lip balm, a book, your phone charger, and more.

181 SORT JEWELRY

If you don't have a designated jewelry box (or if yours is overflowing), the top drawer of your dresser is a great alternative. Line it with velvet fabric and insert shallow acrylic organizers to contain earrings, bracelets, and rings.

182 GET HOOKED ON JEWELRY

If you don't have a spare drawer, hang simple hooks on the wall above your dresser or on either side of your vanity mirror and loop a necklace or bracelet on each. You could also craft a portable option with corkboard tiles and pins in a frame or use a small section of chicken wire or perforated metal to hold earrings.

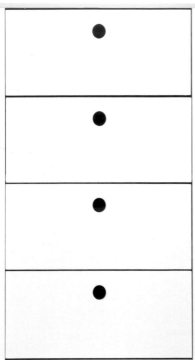

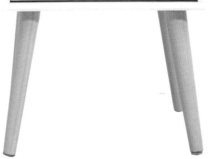

183 DIVIDE DRAWERS

One large drawer may not be suitable for smaller articles of clothing. Using dividers or bins, eliminate drawer chaos by sorting like items into categories (shirts, shorts, tanks, socks, pajamas, and so on). The trick is to fold them all in the same manner and into similar sizes, and then put them away in neat rows, standing up. This is the Konmari method, which will make it much easier to find what you're looking for. Additionally, clothing will remain organized for longer.

184

SHOWCASE YOUR ORGANIZATION

Pick up a small, curved dish for holding your rings—many have a center spike for just this purpose—and keep one on your nightstand and one in the kitchen, so you'll always know where to look. Or repurpose a kitchen item for the dresser top: A tiered serving platter can make for excellent bracelet storage, making the most of little-used vertical space.

185

LET A DESK
DOUBLE AS A VANITY

If you need a multipurpose surface in your bedroom, a floating desk is a space-saving option. The interior of the desk can keep work materials organized, while the top can store perfume, makeup essentials, and the like.

186

KEEP A WORK-LIFE BALANCE

If you keep your desk in your bedroom, move your work materials out of sight at the end of the workday. Keeping work on full display can impact your sleep, especially if you're distracted by paperwork or email when you're not on the clock.

187
HANG AN OVERSIZED MIRROR

A large mirror adds light and dimension, helping a room look and feel bigger. This visual trick makes the most of a small space and is a fun opportunity to infuse a room with your personal style.

188 KEEP AN OPEN MIND

In a small space, don't assume that everything has to be hidden in order to maintain an organized room. As long as everything has a designated spot, you can put things away even while they remain out in the open. For example, open shelving (popular in kitchens and dining rooms) can work in a bedroom too, where you might have stylish wardrobe items that deserve to become part of the décor. Hook your fabulous high heels over picture rails or strips of molding mounted on the wall. Keep your perfume bottles on a decorative tray, or store silk scarves in a colorful, neat stack. If there's no room in the closet, buy a pretty hamper with a cover, or hang one to save floor space. Figure out what works best for your space.

189 OFFER THE HOTEL EXPERIENCE

When setting up a room for guests, you can never go wrong with classic white. Crisp white sheets will make a room feel fresh and welcoming. (For a personal touch, include a decorative blanket.) Add a small bouquet of flowers, branches, or a plant to infuse life into the room.

190 TEMPT WITH LUXURIOUS LINENS

High end bedding like an Egyptian cotton sheet set, especially in white, gives the room a formal, hotel-like feel. Get the highest thread count you can afford and make sure to include at least four pillows.

191 STOCK UP ON TOILETRIES

You never know what your guests may have forgotten, so include everything! Consider disposable razors, shaving cream, toothpaste, toothbrushes, floss, shampoo and conditioner, deodorant, soap, lotion, makeup remover, mouthwash, tampons and pads, comb and brush, and cotton balls and swabs. You can find inexpensive travel-size toiletries at big chain stores or dollar stores. Or, when you stay at a hotel, bring home the extra toiletries and add them to your supply.

192 INCLUDE A HAMPER

Designate a separate hamper just for guest clothes. If it gets full, offer to do a load, or point them to the laundry room if they prefer. Remember, you want to pamper your guests and make them feel as if they're on vacation!

193 TRY SOMETHING NEW

The guest room is an opportunity to explore new design options, so have some fun! Because it's not a 24-7 living space, it's the perfect place to take some décor risks. Try a bold paint color or experiment with color combinations and patterns, as long as your choices feel sleep-friendly and soothing.

194 TRY TWIN BEDS

Depending on how frequently you have guests (and how many you host at a time), consider using two twin beds instead of a full or queen. It adds playfulness to the space, opens up more decorating options, and can be great if you're used to hosting platonic pairs.

195 KEEP AN EYE ON TEMPERATURE

Guests may get too hot or too cold in the middle of the night, so consider the options you can offer them. For chilly evenings, provide an extra-warm blanket; for hot summer nights, a ceiling fan is always a great addition for good airflow. If you can't install a ceiling fan, a small table-top or standing fan will work too.

196 CREATE A GUEST HAVEN

If you live in a small home or don't have a designated bedroom for your guests, you can still pamper them by putting together a guest basket. They'll feel just as cared for on the pull-out sofa bed if they can tell you've prepared and are eager to have them. Offer freshly laundered blankets and sheets, a set of travel-size toiletries, and an extra toothbrush (just in case). If you can, give them a place to keep their things, such as a designated closet or dresser, or set up a luggage rack for their suitcase. An extra chair can perform this job just as well, and will help keep their things from getting underfoot.

197 IMPROVISE A NIGHTSTAND

In a one-bedroom apartment or small space where your guests are sleeping in the living room or den, it can be difficult to provide them with the amenities of a true bedroom. Start with the guest basket (see Item 196) and use a folding tray table, chair, or even a stack of big books to improvise a nightstand. (You can strap the books together with a leather belt or nestle them in a box.) Your guests will need somewhere to put their glasses and charge their phone while they sleep, and they'll appreciate your thoughtfulness!

PLAN A SAFE
KIDS' ROOM

Organizing the kids' room or nursery begins a little differently than for many other rooms—your first focus is safety, then ease of use, and finally, a decorating scheme. Babyproofing is of primary importance, and the process will change as your child grows. Consulting a professional is optimal, but you can get a head start by kneeling down to your child's level to find any sharp edges that need to be padded. Anchor all large furniture in place, and install childproof latches and baby gates where needed. When decorating, choose bedding and window coverings first, and adjust paint colors and accessories to suit.

199 INSTALL UTILITY LIGHTING

The kids' room is the site of many vital tasks, so a variety of lighting options will come in handy. Install a dimmer switch so you're less likely to disturb a sleeping child when you check in at night. Make sure there is ample lighting near rocking chairs and changing tables, and always make sure cords are out of reach of the little ones.

200 LIGHTS OUT

Babies are incredibly sensitive to light, so consider layering blackout shades with regular curtains. Curtains provide a decorative element, while blackout shades provide function, blocking out the sun during nap time.

201 MIX UP THE STORAGE

Large drawers and baskets can make it easy to misplace tiny items in kids' rooms. Look for drawer organizers and bins that take clothing sizes into consideration. A fresh coat of bright paint on an old dresser can make for a brand new piece.

202 USE AN ANTIQUE ARMOIRE FOR BABY

An armoire may seem like a very adult piece of furniture, but an old antique can be fitted up as a perfect closet for baby clothes. Ideal for nurseries that don't have a closet—or have one that's so large it's better suited for storage than swallowing up tiny onesies—an armoire can usually fit multiple racks of pint-sized pieces. You could also use simple tension rods, as small baby clothes don't tend to weigh very much. Remove the doors entirely for neat, open storage (you could even sort all those cute little clothes by color), or leave them on for a surprisingly sophisticated addition to your baby's new abode.

203 SAVE MONEY

Don't spend on a separate changing table and dresser—if your dresser has a large enough surface area, you can buy a dresser-top changing pad to convert it into a changing table. When the baby grows out of diapers, remove the changing pad setup and turn it back into a regular dresser.

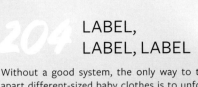

204 LABEL, LABEL, LABEL

Without a good system, the only way to tell apart different-sized baby clothes is to unfold them—and who wants to do that? Label the insides of dresser drawers by clothing type and size. This way, anyone can help with dressing the baby, giving parents a much-needed break.

205
DON'T GO OVERBOARD ON BABY

There's a ton of adorable, tiny baby furniture on the market, but remember that kids will grow out of it quickly. When outfitting a room for a baby, invest in pieces that are high quality and can grow with your child.

206
DESIGN A FUNCTIONAL CHILDREN'S ROOM

After babyhood, your children will develop opinions of their own. When decorating and organizing kids' rooms, make sure to involve them throughout the entire process—from planning to implementation. They need to know that their voices and preferences matter—and it makes a world of difference when it comes to maintaining a clean room later on.

207 ORGANIZE LIKE A CHILD

Get down to your kid's eye level and find out what they see. Can they reach their toys and books? Is everything labeled in an age-appropriate way? For readers, words are fine, but for little kids use pictures or symbols. Make sure you are organizing the space with them in mind.

208 SET THEM UP FOR SUCCESS

Clear out anything that is not being used. Arrange furniture to allow for maximum floor space. Get rid of all visual clutter in the room. Declutter closets, drawers, and toys monthly. Set up a homework station in the bedroom or elsewhere (see Item 295). Keep it simple! Remember, less is more. Hang a calendar (let your children pick it out) over the desk and teach your kids to write in project and homework due dates, after-school activities, and lesson times. Make sure they check their calendars every morning and evening.

209 MAKE A PLAY CORNER

Your kids' interests and passions should extend to their other spaces around the home as well. Play spaces and study corners should reflect their interests—they'll take more pride in these areas, and so will you. If you have younger kids who need supervision and they spend a lot of time with you in common areas of the house (such as the kitchen or home office), it's a good idea to set up a play corner for them in these rooms. Use bins, crates, or lockers to keep a few select toys in this area, and put down a comfy rug or mount some fun wall art to designate the space. This will help them play on their own while you work, cook, or get things done around the house.

210 DON'T OVERCOMMIT TO A THEME

Kids' interests change quickly, so avoid making major themed purchases, like a race car bed or princess-themed wallpaper. Instead, opt for less expensive ways to highlight what they love, like a cute sheet set or a piece of wall art. Smaller elements are easier to swap in and out as your children's hobbies change.

211 KEEP THINGS IN SIGHT

When designing a space for your kids, remember that they'll use it more than you will. Store toys in easy-to-access bins and wire baskets. Consider using clear plastic containers so kids can find what they're looking for without having to ask you. Keep the height of shelving at a kid-friendly level so little hands can reach what they need.

212 LOFT THE BED

Somewhat like a bunk bed, raising your child's bed allows you to maximize space in a smaller bedroom (once your kids are old enough to sleep higher up, of course). Use the area under the lofted bed as an arts-and-crafts area, a reading nook, or a homework space. It's twice the essentials with half the footprint.

213 SNAG A TRUNDLE BED

Providing two beds in the space of one, a trundle bed is a great option for sleepovers. Once kids outgrow the trundle, you can remove the mattress and use the under-bed trundle frame to store miscellaneous items like fresh linens, games, puzzles, and other toys.

214 KEEP ART SUPPLIES NEAR THE CRAFT AREA

If you've ever spilled a tube of glitter on your floor, you know that the less distance craft supplies need to travel, the better. Add storage, like drawers or baskets, underneath the craft area. Organize craft supplies by type to make it easy for kids to put things back on their own.

215 USE LEDGES

Although they're probably most often used to display photos, ledges are also a great storage place for favorite books or small toys. Plus they allow for storage in plain sight, making it easy for young kids to find what they're looking for.

216 DISPLAY YOUR KIDS' ARTWORK

Kids make a ton of artwork—why not put it on exhibit? Use a corkboard to easily hang your children's artwork from school and playtime. Make sure the corkboard is hung high enough so that kids don't get their little hands into pushpins or rip down artwork accidentally. Involve your kids in choosing which artwork to hang, and rotate pieces every few months, just like in a real museum.

217 MAKE KIDS' BOOKS ACCESSIBLE

If you have a large collection of kids' books or just want a sturdy option, the IKEA FLISAT standing bookshelf makes books easy to display and easy for kids to reach (and put back). Plus, the wood comes unfinished, so you can customize the shelf with paint to match the kids' room.

218

PUT TOYS INTO ROTATION

Keep your child interested in their playthings by rotatıng their items in and out, giving them access to their toys a few at a time. Tuck some toys away; then switch in new toys every few weeks. It makes what they already have feel new again, and it cuts down on toy area clutter.

219

TEACH KIDS TO DONATE

Before major holidays or birthdays, work with your child to gather toys that they've outgrown or no longer play with to donate to a nonprofit or other charity drive. Help your child understand that not all kids have the same access to toys and books. When they understand where their old things are going and why, it will be easier to let go.

220 TAME YOUR CLOSET

Your bedroom closet can contain all manner of things: clothes, shoes, bags, and everything else. To keep it organized, take control of the clutter and customize your closet to your specific needs. Make sure to purge beforehand in order to gain valuable space and avoid the headache of organizing things you don't use. After you've cleaned everything out, try to follow the "one in, one out" rule. If you purchase something new, donate something old.

221 SORT OUT YOUR ITEMS

Set aside some time to clear out your bedroom closet and sort through everything in it. Divide into four categories: keep, repair, toss, and donate. Sort through duplicates and purge the older items. Identify a spot for everything. If an item doesn't have a home, make one or purge it.

222 MAXIMIZE YOUR CLOSET SPACE

Purchase matching hangers for a streamlined look. Maximize hanging space with double rods. Some people prefer to hang pants on the top rack and tops on the bottom one. Figure out what suits your needs. Place purses and bags inside each other like nesting dolls. Put out-of-season clothing into a longer-term storage spot.

223 PUT SHOES ON DISPLAY

Shoe clutter is one of the hardest things to get control of—the average woman owns well over twenty pairs! There are endless storage options, so get shoes up off the floor. Display them on a shelf, in see-through bins or neatly arranged in rows. Clear plastic bins keep the dust off and extend the life of shoes—you probably spent a fortune on them, so care for them well!

224 ROLL UP ACCESSORIES

Things like belts, ties, and scarves can be neatly rolled up and placed together in drawer organizers. This is the perfect accessory solution for those of us with small closets. It also extends the life of silk ties, which can suffer indentations from tie hangers.

225 COLOR-CODE CLOTHING

Closet organization doesn't end after you've purged and categorized. Go one step further by color-coding clothing to finish off the space. It's pleasing to the eye and gives the space a more uniform and streamlined look. A color-coded wardrobe also speeds things up when you are picking your outfit for the day. It makes it easier to find what you're looking for, especially when you absolutely must locate that special blue sweater.

226 UTILIZE EVERY SPACE

For those with a limited amount of space, think about how you can use the overlooked areas in your home as storage. Add hooks, shoe bags, or racks to the backs of doors and install high shelves for items you use infrequently. Think creatively about neglected spaces in your home.

227 STORE CLOTHES SEASONALLY

When the seasons change, it's time to pull out the bathing suits and sundresses (or the wool scarves and coats), but unless you have spacious closets, you're going to have to pack up last season's gear to make room for the new items. Remember, the cleaner and more organized your storage, the more pleasant it will be to pull back out next year. Your seasonal storage area must be clean, cool, dark, and dry in order to protect your clothing. Avoid areas near heating systems or moisture to prevent fading or attracting insects. In order to make unpacking a breeze the next season, place all of your sweaters in one container, all your heavy pants in another, coats in a third, and so on. Continue combing through your winter wardrobe until everything has been put away.

228 FIND A PLACE FOR YOUR SEASONAL CLOTHES

Unused suitcases, or even the clear zip-up bags that comforters come in can be repurposed as storage. If you are out of places to hide your boxes or totes, you can stack a few boxes on top of each other and drape a colorful cloth over them, creating an improvised table. Inspect all of your storage containers to make sure they are free from cracks or stains that could allow your clothes to become damaged. You can line your containers with acid-free paper or use cedar chests for storage to keep fabric-chomping insects away. Although you'll want to keep your seasonal wardrobe out of the way, keep in mind that you still want the clothes to be accessible enough so they're not a burden to unpack next season. Some storage containers can easily slide under your bed or couch.

229 DON'T HANG EVERYTHING

Organize your clothing by category to reduce clutter and keep things neat, and then, decide what you should and shouldn't hang. Knit tees, sweaters, and jeans are better off folded. Avoid hanging delicate items like woven sweaters, which can stretch out if hung. Take advantage of drawer space as much as you can.

230 USE THE CLOSET DOOR

If your closet has a swivel door, not an accordion door or sliding one, use over-the-door hooks to hang scarves and belts. These items fit perfectly here because they're long but not bulky, so the door will still shut completely once when you're done dressing.

231 INVEST IN GOOD HANGERS

For the most optimal closet storage, buy thin velvet hangers. They're light, they don't take up a lot of space, and they're non-slip, so your clothes won't slide off of them and onto the floor. Plus, their slim profile reduces the bulky, packed-in look of some closets.

232 TRY A MULTIBAR HANGER

If you're the kind of person who has the same piece of clothing in multiple colors, this is the option for you. Multibar hangers have tiers that clip into one another, creating a waterfall effect. You can always see the top piece of clothing, and the whole group will take up less space on the clothing rack.

233 DON'T BE AFRAID TO GO CUSTOM

If you don't have the closet of your dreams or room for a walk-in, make the space you do have work harder for you. Customizing is a relatively easy DIY project and will allow you to cater to the items you have or wear the most. If you can't go custom, find a good hanging organizer with separate compartments. Set it up alongside your hanging clothing and use it for sweaters, folded pants, or accessories.

234 LET GO OF CLOTHES YOU DON'T WEAR

Try this if you have a hard time parting with clothing. Place clothes that you haven't recently worn in a bag, but don't give them away just yet. If you find yourself digging through the bag for certain items, return them to your closet. Items that remain untouched in the bag after a month or two get donated.

235 TIDY UP KIDS' CLOSETS

Make it a habit to tidy up kids' closets on a weekly basis. Tidying allows the kids to see what's clean, what's dirty, and what they might want to put together as outfits for the week ahead. Reorganize clothing into categories and hang like items together. Rehang clothes that have fallen off the hangers. Straighten up shoes and accessories. Move sports equipment to the garage or mudroom and winter coats, outerwear, and other gear to the hall closet. Assess the need for clothing, shoes, and accessories often. Haul away anything that is no longer being used.

236
KEEP TINY SHOES ORGANIZED

Designate a space in the closet for your child's shoes. Depending on the children's ages (and heights), it can be a shelf, door organizer, or basket on the floor. Make sure there is enough room to fit all of the shoes each child owns. Teach them to put their shoes away each day and to tidy them weekly.

237
CONTAIN ACCESSORIES

Belts, bags, hair accessories, and hats can become a whirlwind of clutter in a child's closet. Corral these accessories in baskets or clear shoe boxes and label each clearly. Another method is to hang wall hooks on the sides of the closet for belts and bags. There are also special hat hangers that can really help out. Keep everything off of the floor (with the exception of a shoe basket) to minimize clutter and keep the closet looking tidy.

238 PERFORM A SEASONAL SWEEP

Remove all out-of-season clothing from the closet. Assess each item's size, condition, and whether your child still needs it. Label a bin with your child's name, the sizes that are being stored in the box, and the season. Launder everything and store the bin on the top shelf of the closet or in the attic. If anything is needed, you'll know where to find it—and if it's not needed, you can move it to the donation pile or hand it down to the next recipient.

239

CLEAN, PURGE, AND SET A SYSTEM FOR YOUR LINEN CLOSET

Ideally your linen closet will be organized into easily viewable and reachable sections. You'll want to first stand back and observe the current organizational system you have in place. Is there order—or is there chaos? Does it work for you? Setting up a system with functional organization in mind helps keep things tidy without a lot of effort. Next, clear out the closet and start with a fresh canvas. Vacuum and wipe down shelving, walls, and baseboards. Toss or donate things you no longer use and set limits on existing items. Keep only three sets of sheets per bed and three towels and washcloths per person in the household.

240 LABEL AND COLOR-CODE TO YOUR ADVANTAGE

Using a label maker or tags, create categories. Designate where you are going to place your linens so all family members know where to find things and can put items away with minimal guidance. Labeling also helps keep closets neat and streamlines the space. Here are some categories that can be used in the linen closet: towels, sheet sets, winter bedding, throw blankets, quilts, pillows, curtains, table linens. You can also color-code linens for different areas of the house. For example, assign white for guest towels and gray or blue for family towels.

241 FOLD LIKE A PRO

There are many folding methods that work. Whichever method you choose, remain consistent. Fold all towels and bedding the same way. By doing this, the closet will become more space-efficient and tidy.

242 FOLD A FITTED SHEET

Folding a fitted sheet is not as hard as it seems. For true perfection, do this on a flat surface, but you can do it standing too. First, tuck your hands into the pockets of two corners, one hand per pocket. Bring your hands together and flip one corner over the other so they nest. Do the same with the other corners, so all four are now nested. Now treat the nested corners like a point and fold normally. Viola!

243 MAKE SURE SHELVES ADJUST

If possible, consider installing adjustable linen closet shelving. Because the items that go into linen closets are stackable and don't need to hang, a closet with adjustable shelving can make a big difference. You can DIY this with relative ease by installing removable pegs to change the height of shelves whenever you need.

MAKE SURE LINENS SMELL FRESH

After doing laundry, make sure your linens are completely dry before folding and putting them away. Any lingering moisture trapped in the folds can make a whole shelf of sheets or towels smell like mildew and must. Try tucking a small herb or floral sachet in with each sheet set to add a nice additional scent.

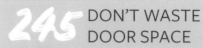 ## DON'T WASTE DOOR SPACE

Maximize storage space on the back of the linen closet door by investing in a screw-in, multitiered, compact wire basket unit. Here you can place odds and ends like extra lotions, shampoos and conditioners, soaps, and cleaning supplies.

 ## DESIGNATE GUEST TOWELS

No one wants to do a last-minute load of laundry just before visitors arrive. Designate a set of towels for guests only (it helps to pick one color, for ease of organizing). They'll stay pristine and fluffy, and you won't have to worry about scrambling to accommodate unexpected guests.

247

KEEP SMALL TOWELS SEPARATE

Washcloths and hand towels can get lost in the shuffle; store them separately from large towels so they're easy to find. Fold these smaller towels into squares and store them in neat stacks. They can share a shelf with backup items such as extra paper towels, tissues, and toilet paper.

248

GROUP SHEETS BY BED

Don't separate bedsheets into fitted, flat, and duvet. Instead, sort them into sets that facilitate making the bed. A set might include a fitted sheet, a flat sheet, and two pillowcases. This makes it easy to see which sheets you have available for each bed, and when you need to change the sheets, you can grab the set and go.

249

NEST SHEETS IN PILLOWCASES

Use pillowcases or shams as handy storage for their corresponding sheet sets. Put folded sheets at the bottom of the pillowcase, and then fold neatly in half and stack. If you have mismatched sheets, use a label and a clothespin to specify which sheets are inside.

250

KEEP YOUR
BATHROOMS CLEAN

Being organized doesn't just mean clearing the clutter from drawers and closets. It also means implementing a daily and weekly cleaning routine. Get into the habit of quickly cleaning the bathroom each morning after you've gotten ready for the day. It only takes a few minutes and it's well worth the time and minimal effort. When you return home in the evening, your clean bathroom will be calling your name—perhaps to indulge in a stress-relieving bubble bath.

251 PRACTICE THESE HABITS DAILY

Wipe counters and sinks. Quickly mop up any toothpaste messes or countertop mishaps, and remove the toiletry clutter that's bound to accumulate. Put dirty clothes in the hamper. Keep your sinks, toilets, and showers clean daily with the natural cleaning solutions found in Item 272.

252

EMPTY THE TRASH IF NEEDED

Don't necessarily wait until the trash is full before emptying it as with other rooms. Bathroom trash cans may not fill as quickly as some others, but they can be full of messy or bulky things like sticky containers.

253 THINK ABOUT PROXIMITY

Placement is key when keeping the bathroom clean. Place the daily shower cleaner in the shower, the toilet cleaner near the toilet, and the sink cleaner below the sink. If it's close by, you're more likely to use it.

254 KEEP IT FRESH WITH ESSENTIAL OILS

Keep your lavatory smelling fresh by adding a few drops of pure essential oil to a cup of baking soda and placing it behind the toilet. You can also add a few drops to the inside of the cardboard toilet paper roll each time you change it. Finally, add a drop to the trash can when changing the bag. Essential oils work like a charm, and they're much better than chemicals.

255 STOCK EXTRA TOILET PAPER CREATIVELY

Don't hide extra toilet paper under the sink. If more toilet paper is visible, your family and guests will be more likely to replace an empty roll on the toilet paper holder. Consider using a tall glass vase or a basket to make extra rolls look more appealing.

256 KEEP A PLUNGER HANDY

If you have guests coming over, make sure there's a plunger (and plenty of toilet paper) in the bathroom. You don't want your guests to get caught without one when they need it—it's embarrassing and unpleasant for both of you.

257

KEEP EXTRA TOWELS OUTSIDE THE BATHROOM

Moisture can work against you in the bathroom, and excess moisture can make linens smell musty or even mildewy. Folded towels are a particular risk since they can't dry out fully. Store folded towels in a linen closet or bedroom and bring them to the bathroom as needed.

258

INCORPORATE PLANTS

Take advantage of the moisture in your bathroom and add plants that thrive in wet environments. Plants in the fern family will do well in a humid bathroom, and they'll look beautiful too—so you'll both be happy.

259 LIGHTEN UP

Some people intentionally go for dark, bold colors in a small space to make a dramatic statement, but your best bet for maximizing space is a soft, light palette, with just a few pops of color. Use your towels and a few small pieces of art to add zing to an otherwise serene color scheme. Natural light always makes a space seem bigger, but if you can't bring sunshine in, use accent lighting with natural-spectrum bulbs. A fixture swap can make a big difference: Think about wall-mounted sconces on either side of a vanity. And if you have a single fixture, find something fresh for the spot that reflects your personal style.

 **GET
CLEAR**

Introduce as much glass and as many reflective surfaces as you can to open up your space. Swapping out an old-fashioned opaque shower stall or shower curtain for a sheet of clear glass can make an amazing difference (and force you to keep that shower sparkly clean!). Maximize your mirrors, too—just don't install one directly across from the commode.

**261 PURGE THE
CLUTTER**

Go through every single thing in your bathroom and determine whether or not you really need it. Be ruthless. No matter how expensive that moisturizer was, if you don't use it, it goes out. Look at expiration dates and ditch anything past its prime. Keep only the items you need. For things like cotton swabs and cotton balls, store the big packages in a closet and keep just a handful in the bathroom, in small containers.

262 LOSE THE CABINETS

Open shelving takes up less space than cabinets. If your towels are color coordinated, they add to the décor. Special shelving racks that fit over the commode make use of often-ignored space. And a slim shelf (such as a spice rack) might be a perfect solution for toiletries. Use basket and bins to contain any items you don't want on permanent display. Another trick is to use a storage ladder, which adds a fun, contemporary feel and allows you to customize how and where to stash items you need.

263 USE ALL DOORS

Use all available doors for storage—hang towels on the back of the entry door, and store the hair dryer on the back of the cabinet door. Use adhesive hooks or over-the-door systems to hang your robe or towels. You can also hang a mesh shoe organizer over the door. These inexpensive organizers work great for bottles, cleaners, and brushes.

264 GO GREEN WITH SOAP

Invest in a refillable glass soap dispenser—it looks pretty on the sink top and is easy to refill with your favorite liquid hand soap purchased in bulk. Plus, you cut down on single-use plastics—it's a win-win!

265
USE METAL WITH CAUTION

It's not uncommon for metal baskets and organizers to get rusty over time, especially in the high-moisture environment of a bathroom. When you're searching for bathroom caddies and organizers, look for stainless steel, bamboo, or plastic options.

266
ADD A PLEASANT SCENT

For a luxurious feel, hang a bundle of eucalyptus behind your showerhead, so it's out of the way of water and nestled against the shower wall. Steam from the shower will create an incredible aroma, and it looks elegant too!

267 HANG A SHOWER CURTAIN

An outdated tub or shower can be easily dressed up with a stylish shower curtain. After using the shower, close the curtain fully to allow the folds in the liner to dry, preventing mold or mildew.

268 HANG BATHROOM ART WISELY

Avoid hanging irreplaceable art or photographs in the bathroom. Moisture can quickly damage even framed pieces—for special items in your collection, it's just not worth the risk.

269 CONSIDER A STYLING CADDY

Give hairbrushes and other styling tools a home in an easy-to-move caddy stored underneath your bathroom sink. It can transition from under the sink to the counter quickly, but it's easy to pack and stow away to prevent clutter. Using a silicone mat for hot tools helps keep your bathroom countertop safe from heat damage.

270 CORRAL YOUR MEDICINE CABINET

How many of us have opened our medicine cabinet to be greeted by a cascade of falling pill bottles, loose Band-Aids, and the like? Prevent this by storing stray items in small acrylic boxes by category. Using clear shelf dividers can double your space. Be careful when storing medication in the bathroom—for tips, see Item 071.

271 KEEP BATHROOM CLOSETS NEAT

The bathroom closet might be solely used to store personal care products. Contain products using clear shoe boxes and labels. Corral these categories: first aid, ice packs and heating pads, nail care, travel accessories, dental, shaving, lotions, cotton swaps, tampons and pads, hair care, and bath items.

272 MAKE YOUR OWN NATURAL CLEANERS

Household essentials such as baking soda and vinegar have a wide variety of applications, including as natural cleaners. Follow these instructions to make and use homemade cleaning solutions for your bathroom. Be careful not to use vinegar on natural stone or oil-rubbed bronze fixtures, as it can damage porous stone and finishes.

NATURAL SINK CLEANER Sprinkle baking soda around the sink interior and scrub with a wet sponge. Or mix a solution of 1 cup vinegar, 2 cups water, and 10 drops lemon or lavender essential oil to create a multipurpose cleaner.

NATURAL SHOWER CLEANER Use a damp cloth soaked with vinegar to clean shower doors. Finish with a dry microfiber cloth. Scrub shower walls with a wet sponge covered with essential oil–infused baking soda to loosen soap scum. Add a drop of liquid Castile soap for extra cleaning power. You can also make a divine-smelling daily shower cleaner by mixing together 1 cup vinegar, 2 cups water, $\frac{1}{2}$ cup rubbing alcohol, 10 drops peppermint essential oil, and 10 drops orange essential oil in a spray bottle. Spray down showers daily to keep soap scum at bay. For best results, begin with a clean shower when using a daily cleaner.

NATURAL TOILET CLEANER Sprinkle baking soda into the toilet, spray a generous amount of full-strength vinegar around the toilet bowl, and let it sit for several minutes. Scrub with a toilet brush. You can also use an old pumice stone—it works great for toilet stains.

273 CLEAN SMARTER, NOT HARDER

Keeping your bathroom properly ventilated will save you time cleaning long term. Run the fan while you're in the shower and keep the bathroom door open post-shower or bath to let out moisture. This will cut down on mildew growth, meaning less scrubbing later. When you use your toilet brush, rinse it and then position the handle between the toilet seat and the bowl, with the brush hanging over the bowl to dry. This will prevent the brush from retaining bacteria, so you won't have to buy a new one multiple times a year.

274 USE ROLL-AWAY STORAGE
WITH A PEDESTAL SINK

A pedestal sink might seem like a storage dead zone, but tucking a roll-away organizer underneath can be a game changer. It provides plenty of drawers for frequently used toiletries, but you can remove it from the bathroom if you have guests visiting or just need more space.

275 CREATE ZONES IN YOUR OFFICE

The home office is a versatile and multiuse work-horse of a room, responsible for everything from bills to day jobs to blogger duties! With so much going on and the amount of time you're likely to spend in this space, you'll want to set up an organized room that will stay that way. Divide your space into several zones: work, mail, bill payment, filing, office supply, planning, books, and school.

276 LET YOUR SPACE DO THE WORK

Your work zone will be at your desk. It includes your computer, lamp, printer, tax organizer, and desktop files (your most-used papers that don't stay in a drawer long enough to live there). Your mail zone and bill zone live nearby. The mail area should include bins for incoming and outgoing mail, as well as stamps, envelopes, address labels, packing tape, a postage scale, a stationery set, and any other correspondence needs. All things needed to pay bills go in the bill payment zone. This likely includes the bills themselves, a calculator, your checks, a budget binder, and an account and password log.

277 FILE THE PAPERS AND SUPPLIES AWAY

Your filing cabinet (a paragon of home organization!) goes in the filing zone, as expected. Your office supply zone holds extra printer paper, printer ink, pens and pencils, staples, paper clips, binder clips, tape, file folders, labeler and label tape, and other office needs.

278 MISCELLANEOUS ZONES

The planning zone provides a home for any family calendars, personal organizers or planners, and related supplies (extra inserts, stickers, washi tape, etc.). Professional and business books should have their own space in your office. And don't forget the kids! The school zone includes any school paperwork and can also incorporate a homework station (see Item 295).

279 ENJOY A POCKET-SIZED OFFICE SPACE

If your home office shares space with another room or sometimes has to serve another function, make the space as versatile as it needs to be. Use labeled baskets to store supplies and paperwork and place them under your desk or on a shelf for easy but convenient access.

280 PAY ATTENTION TO DESK PLACEMENT

Believe it or not, where you place your desk in your office can impact your productivity. You might find you don't like to work with your back to the door—it makes some people feel anxious or uneasy. Likewise, you might not like to face a window if it gets too much sunlight and is too hot in the late afternoon. Try a few different placements for your desk and see what works for you.

281

GIVE YOURSELF THE BEST SEAT IN THE HOUSE

You'll probably sit in your desk chair more than any other chair you own, so invest in one that supports your back and spine. The height of your chair should be adjustable and should allow your feet to rest flat on the floor or on a footrest while you work. Your thighs should be parallel to the floor, and your arms should rest gently on the chair's armrests with your shoulders relaxed.

282

ORGANIZE DESK DRAWERS FROM THE INSIDE OUT

We all know the annoyance of arranging your desk supplies and closing the drawer, only to have everything slide around immediately. To avoid this, use adhesive mounting putty to secure small boxes or desk organizers inside your drawers. Mounting putty is removable, making repositioning a breeze.

283 CONSIDER A "MURPHY DESK"

"Murphy desk" might not be a technical term, but you get the idea—a small desk that folds up to fit into a cabinet or closet (or folds up and hooks to the wall) will help to save space in a small room, a shared office, or an apartment.

284 CONTROL PAPER CLUTTER

Paper clutter is the number one problem of messy home offices and it can be overwhelming and daunting to tackle. But once you get a handle on it, curbing paper clutter is a breeze. Take control of incoming paper with a daily system. You should always immediately recycle or shred any junk mail. When bills come in, either pay them right away or place them in a bill organizer. If you deem a paper keepsake worthy, place it in a designated box (see Item 288). Important papers that need to be filed should go into a "to file" folder—but only if you don't have time to file them right away. Then, once a week, go through and file everything in this folder in its proper place.

285 KEEP A HANDLE ON SCHOOL

School papers can take over your home in an instant. Prevent this from happening by taking five minutes each afternoon, as soon as the kids get home from school, to go through each of their backpacks. Respond to items that need your attention, recycle trash, file artwork (see Item 288), and make sure kids are aware of any homework.

286 STAY CURRENT

Keep only the most current periodicals in your home. If you get a physical newspaper, read it each day and then place it in a designated recycling basket. If you don't have time to read it, recycle it—it's old news. Once a new magazine arrives in the mail, toss the previous edition.

287 TACKLE YOUR TO-DO ITEMS

Anything that needs your attention or response should go into an action folder. Once or twice a week, go through the folder and do what needs doing.

288 CREATE A KEEPSAKE BOX

When you have kids, the artwork, paperwork, pictures, and keepsakes are guaranteed to pile up. You want to wrap up their memories and cherish them forever, but it can be difficult to keep it all corralled and organized. It's essential to set up an organized system so you can file away the keepsakes in an orderly fashion. Assign a large filing box with a lid for each child and add and label as many file folders as you need for the different categories (such as birthday cards, report cards, artwork, grade levels, academic awards, sports, etc.). As years pass, you'll be able to look back through the memories with ease—and the good stuff won't be lost in the shuffle. Be mindful about what you save; not every doodle or art project should make this save pile!

289 ORGANIZE YOUR FILES

If you are the type of person who likes the feel of thumbing through papers and filing away work, you'll appreciate a well-organized filing system. If, instead, you are up to speed on digital record-keeping and own a document scanner, then digital organization is the way to go. Whichever you choose, keep a handle on paperwork by taking action as soon as it arrives. Look over all documents and statements to make sure they are correct. Then shred anything you have online access to, or file away those items that you want to keep on hand. Set up a filing system using color-coded hanging folders and maintain it by purging irrelevant documents at least once a year (before tax season is a good time).

290 CREATE DIY STORAGE BOXES

Pretty boxes, baskets, and organizing bins can get pricey. Consider covering cardboard gift boxes or recyclable containers with decorative paper and using them for storage instead—most rectangular boxes can be wrapped just like a gift, so it's an easy DIY. For a cleaner finish, use double-sided tape.

291 PURGE SUPPLIES YOU DON'T NEED

Do you need a hundred pens? Or will twenty good pens suffice? What about four different kinds of white-out or that kitschy tape dispenser that doesn't really work? Assess what you need and what you really use on a day-to-day basis and donate the rest.

292

TRY PEGBOARDS AND WALL ORGANIZERS

Hanging things on the wall, and over your desk in particular, is a convenient option for office spaces that are short on storage. Peg boards accommodate several elements, like clip-on hanging containers and paper organizers, that are as cute as they are functional.

293

STASH YOUR PRINTER

Many printers are quite bulky, so if you just need a standard black-and-white printer, consider getting a small, compact model. If you need a larger printer with more advanced features, store it somewhere inconspicuous and out of the way, such as under a desk or on the bottom shelf of a bookcase.

294 HIRE A LAZY SUSAN

This handy spinning kitchen organizer can function well in an office setting too. Fill a small one with your most-used office supplies and keep it on a desk or shelf for quick access. You'll be glad to no longer be knocking over your pen cup while reaching for your stapler.

QUICK TIP

TRACK YOUR TAXES

Create file folders to keep track of your taxes during the year. Place the file folders in a mobile file box and keep the box within arm's reach of your work area. If it's out of sight, unfiled paper will surely pile up, so placement is key!

295 CREATE A HOMEWORK CENTER

A homework station is a great idea if you have school-aged children. It allows them to complete their schoolwork and study for upcoming tests in a comfortable and quiet area and work on any projects with all of the necessary tools at their disposal. Set up the desk against a wall or window with good light. Make sure there are enough power outlets for all the electronics and that the chair can move easily on the floor surface. Set up a few cubbies, paper trays, and stacking pencil cases to hold extra supplies and keep things as tidy as possible. Keep in mind that each child works differently—some kids like to be where their parents are and others need their own space.

BINDER IT

Take ten minutes to create a parent's school binder to keep track of important paperwork needed throughout the year. Make a separate tab for each of the following: school calendar, school information (address, phone number, principal, etc.), teacher information (name, phone number, email address, etc.), lunch schedules, bell schedules, bus schedules, sick notes, handbook and policies. You could also choose to use a folder instead of a binder.

296 LOCK IN A LIBRARY

For the bookworms out there, an at-home library is a dream come true—and it doesn't necessarily require a free room. All you need is a corner of an office (or living room, or even hallway), a few pieces of furniture, and your favorite books. Place two (or more) matching bookshelves against an empty bit of wall, tuck them behind a sofa, nestle them into a corner, or mount open shelving on an odd wall space. Plop your comfiest armchair next to a bright, focused floor lamp or set up a small table and a few chairs for a work surface. In a small home, mount narrow shelves in a long hallway and add a window seat for a space-saving option. Now it's time to settle in and get lost in a favorite!

297 CORRAL CRAFT SUPPLIES

Crafting supplies are one of the hardest things to organize and keep organized. If you're lucky enough to have a designated craft room, you've fought half the battle by carving out the space—but either way, you're probably dealing with piles of scrapbook paper, yarn, sewing patterns, art supplies, or quilting fabric. Get control of your supplies by purging what you no longer use and implementing a category system for the rest. Whether you have an entire room or simply a closet, the process will be the same. You'll start by clearing out the space entirely: Purge what you don't need and then clean up the space. After you've cleaned, set up your systems and containerize! You can use whatever suits your fancy (mason jars, filing cabinets, bins, etc.). Once your categories are set, label the containers and put everything away.

GIFT WRAP
TO GO

For many people a gift wrap station isn't possible. Thankfully, organizing retailers like The Container Store stock small, space-friendly, and portable options that can fit neatly inside a closet. These organizers keep all of your wrapping supplies corralled without taking up a ton of space. Just remember to clearly label each of your categories: ribbons and bows; tapes, scissors, and glue; pens and markers; gift bags; and tissue paper. Store those gangly wrapping paper rolls in a drawer, a long narrow plastic bin, or a plastic organizer. A spare trash can, basket, or umbrella stand can also work wonders.

299 CREATE A TINY HOME OFFICE

In even the smallest home, the creative problem-solver can find some office space. Think about what you need—will you be using the area to pay bills and check email, or to run a home-based business? The first can be done in very little space, but anything's possible. You could set up your office in the guest room and keep desktop items minimal so that it's easy to clear out when company arrives. A hall that's long and not too narrow can probably accommodate a slim desk and some storage bins. The desk chair tends to be the thing most likely to get in the way, so use an easy-to-tuck-away stool or borrow a kitchen chair when needed.

300 RETHINK YOUR SPACES

Think about underutilized corners in your home. You can set up a small desk facing into a corner and use vertical space (hanging racks, floating shelves) to minimize the footprint. If there are odd nooks or alcoves, you could fit a small desk and some vertical storage into one of these spaces and hang a curtain over it when not in use. And if you don't have a nook, make your own by removing the rod from a closet. Then you can close the door and hide your office away when not in use.

QUICK TIP

LET IT ROLL

Consider using a rolling storage unit with an attractive wood top as a mobile office. You can store your supplies in it, use the top as a desk when needed, then stash it all and roll the unit to the living room to use as an end table.

301 ORGANIZE THE KIDS' PLAY SPACE

Kids love to have their own space, and organizing their play space is a perfect activity to do together. Since it involves their toys and their designated space, they'll want to be part of the process. And in addition to teaching them the value of cleaning up after themselves, it's a great opportunity for learning activities such as sorting, counting, sharing, and grouping.

DESIGNATE ACTIVITY STATIONS

Set up an easel and paints on an easy-to-mop floor, put games on a table surrounded by cushions, and clear a flat surface for playing with blocks. Think about how the space will be used and plan accordingly.

303 STORE
ACCORDING TO AGE

Younger children like to open bins and boxes on the floor or low shelves, while older children can use drawers, higher shelves, and closets. Try to keep everything within easy reach and avoid boxes that are too large. Toys buried at the bottom of a bin can't be seen and rarely get played with. This is also a great opportunity to instill the love of labels at a young age! For kids who can't read yet, use photographs or illustrations of a container's contents. When your child can see what's supposed to go in the box, they're more likely to put it in the right place.

304 USE LIDS

Sometimes, without lids, when it's time to clean up, kids will just throw toys into the closest bin, not the designated one, and soon the containers are overflowing. You can find boxes with lids just about anywhere, and this small investment will save you much time in the future.

305 KEEP BOXES AROUND THE HOUSE FOR EASY TRANSFERS

Even if you are fortunate enough to have a separate area where your kids play, toys have a way of showing up in the darndest places. Keeping a bin handy will make the nightly toy roundup a snap.

306

HAVE A NIGHTLY CLEAN-UP PARTY

Children need to be shown that cleaning up isn't a chore—it's another way of having fun. Put on a favorite song and have the kids gather and put away toys until it's over; or, while watching a favorite show, have them race to clean up during the commercials. Turning cleanup into a fun activity will help give children pride in their space and establish a routine.

307 KEEP THINGS TIDY

Check the toy bins about once a month. No matter what you do or how many lids you have, a stray toy or two will inevitably get thrown into the wrong bin—and before you know it, the box labeled Barbies is now everything but Barbies.

308 PIECE THE PUZZLES

Puzzles can get out of control so quickly—and the many sizes of boxes can be a pain to organize. To keep things stackable (and help prevent lost pieces!), grab some small, lidded containers and transfer each puzzle to its own one. Cut out the puzzle image from the box (there's usually a small one as well as the big cover shot) and throw it in with the puzzle pieces or tape it to the lid.

309 ASSEMBLE A PLAY TABLE

If you're short on space but want a place for your kids to play with art supplies, puzzles, and games on their own, use flat-topped rolling storage cubes to create a piece-by-piece table. You can attach casters to existing storage cubes or grab some wheeled ones. Make sure there are no overhanging lips or raised details that will prevent them from aligning smoothly. Attach some heavy-duty Velcro strips to the corresponding sides of each cube and put some brightly colored labels on the four corners that will meet in the middle. Store the cubes along the perimeter of the room when not in use—they can hold games, bins, or books—and roll them together when your kids want a workspace.

310 NET A ZOO

A homemade or store-bought hammock is the perfect place to keep stuffed animals—it makes it easy to put away the toys (don't hang it too high!) and it feels like a home or bed where the animals go to sleep at night. If you're a knitter, whip one up with some spare yarn and chunky needles, or simply string up some spare fabric or tulle in a storage corner. You'll save valuable floor space to boot.

311 PITCH A TENT

If your home doesn't have a separate room available for all of the Legos, games, dolls, puzzles, and everything else, there are plenty of ways to separate out some kid-owned space. One enchanting method is to rig up a tent in a corner of the living room, den, bedroom, or even office—wherever you have the floor space. Purchase a premade model or simply stretch some lightweight fabric between a couple of extra chairs and add colorful streamers or fabric strips. String up some battery-powered LED twinkle lights (that don't get hot) for extra charm. Now you have a cozy play space for young kids, and it will keep toys and accessories neatly tucked away and out of sight.

QUICK TIP

LEARN YOUR ABCS

If you have preschool-age children and enough storage space, round up twenty-six bins and label each with a letter of the alphabet and sort toys accordingly. It's a learning tool and organizational system in one!

312 KEEP DIRTY CLOTHES IN HAMPERS

Is your laundry room (or closet or corner) a catch-all place? It's time to get organized, right down to the dust bunnies. Wherever your washer and dryer live, the space should be clutter free and functional. Try not to keep piles of laundry in the laundry area. Instead, keep hampers in each bathroom or bedroom and bring them in when it's laundry day.

313 STORE OTHER HOUSEHOLD ITEMS

If you store other household items in the laundry area, stay organized by keeping them in containers, labeling them, and revisiting them every so often to keep them in check. Some items that might live in this space: tissues, paper towels, toilet paper, sewing items, lightbulbs, tools, cat litter, cleaning wipes, floor cleaners, laundry detergent, soaps, and dryer sheets.

314

THINK OUTSIDE THE SHOE BOX

An over-the-door shoe organizer can hold so much more than shoes. It's perfect for stashing spray bottles and cleaners—keeping them out of the way but still visible so you always know what you have. Plus, you can keep dangerous chemicals out of reach. In the slim space behind the door, store your broom, mop, dusters, and ironing board, along with all your ironing supplies.

315 SET UP FORGET-ME-NOTS

Set up a few baskets or containers to hold lost items found in pockets and left behind in the dryer. Give them some labels so your family always knows where to find the lost coins, lip balms, and buttons.

316 BEAUTIFY YOUR SPACE

Your laundry area should put a smile on your face. Glass apothecary jars with lids are a great option for storing bulk detergent tablets, pods, and powders—they are visually appealing and allow you to see how much soap you have left. Consider painting the space a bright color or outfitting it with cheeky laundry-themed artwork.

317 INCLUDE HOOKS

A set of hooks is a good investment for your laundry area. They will allow you to hang sweaty or damp items like workout clothes and towels, preventing a whole laundry basket of clothes from growing mildew.

318 WASH WITH CARE

If you really want your laundry area to be a haven, decorate it! Adding personal touches such as a family photograph can brighten the space. Organization and efficiency will only be aided by your enjoyment of the room as a whole. You're making it more usable by making it a place you want to be (and maybe laundry won't feel like such a chore for other family members, too).

319 SIMPLIFY THE LAUNDRY SYSTEM

If your laundry sorting process is too compli-
cated, your less-cleaning-inclined family members won't do it properly. Make it easy by clearly
labeling hampers or bins—one for white clothes,
one for dark clothes, one for delicates and hand-
washing, and one for dry cleaning.

320 PREVENT DRYER DISASTERS

On some machines, you can use a dry-erase
marker to jot a quick note to yourself about
which items shouldn't go into the dryer. A
simple "blue sweater" will remind you when
switching loads to fish out that delicate
blend. Test the marker on an inconspicuous
part of your machine first!

321 SET UP A HOME GYM

If you don't have time to drive to the gym or you keep making excuses about why you never go, try setting up a gym in your home. It takes less effort than you'd think to squeeze in some exercise. You only need a few things—and you can use as few or as many of these supplies as you want: towels, yoga supplies, weights, resistance bands, whiteboard (to jot down your workout schedule), speakers, a stand for your phone for playing videos or music.

DEAL WITH GYM ODORS

The major problem with a home gym is the funk! Here are a few tips to keep in mind: Wear antiperspirant; it prevents sweating and reduces moisture. Wash your workout clothes as soon as you're finished. If your clothes really stink, soak them in vinegar before washing. Air shoes out after workouts and wash monthly. Open windows to let fresh air in.

322 STOCK YOUR GYM BAG

If you don't have the luxury of a room specifically for workouts, you can take it with you via a well-stocked gym bag. You'll need these essentials when you're on the go, so keep them neatly organized and accessible in the same place. And make sure used clothes go into the laundry right away! Keep these items in your bag: gym shoes and extra socks; antiperspirant; travel-size bodywash, shampoo, and shower shoes; towel and washcloth; reusable water bottle; disposable bags for stinky gym clothes; earbuds; extra set of clothes; protein bar; sweat towel; hair ties and brush; lifting gloves.

323 KEEP IT SIMPLE

If you don't have room for a treadmill, elliptical, or other piece of machinery, you'll be surprised at the kind of workout you can get using just a few resistance bands. They offer many of the same benefits as weight training, but they're a lot lighter, making them easier to move around the house or throw into a gym bag. They'll cut down on your equipment needs, and you can store them almost anywhere—hang them on the wall behind a door, fold them into a box, or keep them permanently in your duffel bag. The possibilities are endless—and you might find you have room for an organized, efficient home gym after all.

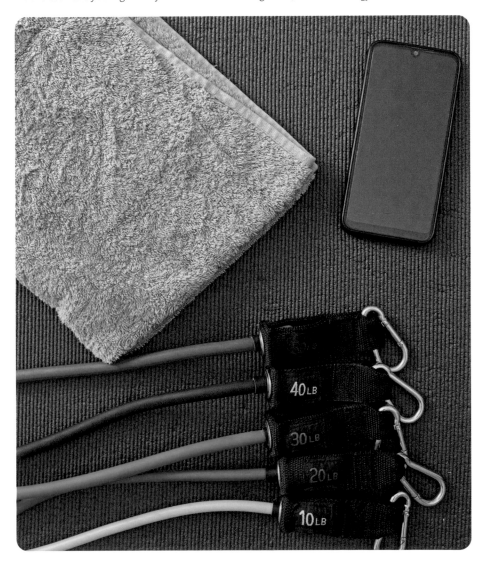

324   LEAN IN

Attics are a blank slate for any new system, won't get in anyone's way, and are good for long-term storage—in short, an organizer's dream come true! If you have an attic with sloped ceilings or triangular spaces under the eaves, you can purchase (or create) specially designed storage bins with slanted sides to fit into these tricky spaces. Some can even be built into the wall or ceiling to provide extra drawer and cubby storage solutions.

325 EMBRACE PLASTIC

Cardboard boxes, even the sturdy ones, will lose their shape and become damaged with frequent use. Instead, choose sturdy plastic containers, which provide a better seal and are easy to move from place to place. If you store holiday decorations in your attic, maintain a separate section for their annual usage.

326 USE THE BEAMS

Those pesky exposed beams across the ceiling and up the walls can actually provide useful, efficient storage space. Make them work for you as shelves for books, which will benefit from being in the dark environment of many attics.

327 BEAUTIFY YOUR ATTIC

If your attic gets good light, let it in, clean up the space, and repaint. If the room looks and feels inviting, you are less likely to fill it with clutter, and you've added a new room to your house! Some attics may require a little more sweat and effort, but there's nothing like turning an unused, dusty space into a cute, useful area for your family.

328   PARE DOWN POSTERITY

Kids' art projects, old school books, former hobbies, unused sports equipment—it all finds a home in the attic. To keep the hoarding tendencies at bay, sort through the whole kit and caboodle and be strict with yourself. Keep only important items with real sentimental value. Plan to properly archive these (which you should do now) or pass them down to the next generation. This will restrict your keepers to family heirlooms and select art or school projects that really reflect their creator (if you can't put them in a book and page through them in one sitting, there are too many!).

329   TOSS, DONATE, OR CONSIGN

Get rid of any damaged items that a local thrift store or donation station wouldn't accept. If they won't accept an item, then you shouldn't either. Donate anything you no longer use but that someone else might enjoy. Consigning is a project in itself, so if you don't have the time to devote, simply donate those things as well. You'll make someone's day when they grab it as a bargain.

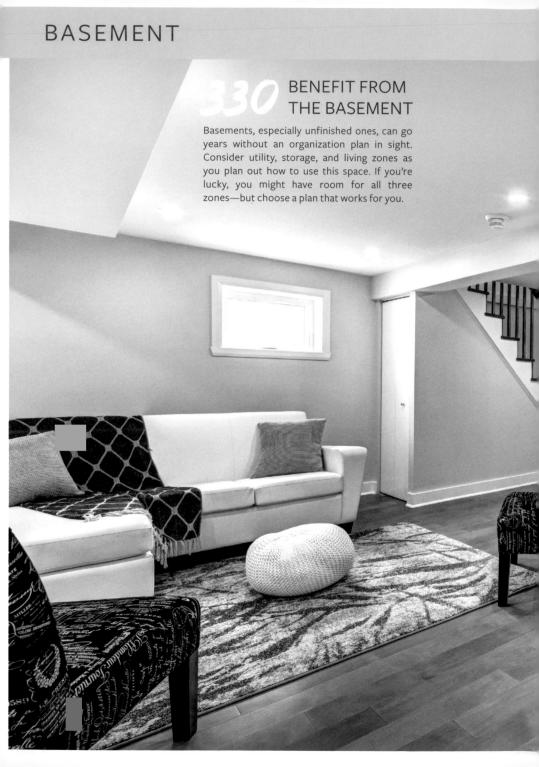

330 BENEFIT FROM THE BASEMENT

Basements, especially unfinished ones, can go years without an organization plan in sight. Consider utility, storage, and living zones as you plan out how to use this space. If you're lucky, you might have room for all three zones—but choose a plan that works for you.

331 KEEP THE UTILITY ZONE ACCESSIBLE

The utility zone of your basement is where the essential basement fixtures are located: the furnace, water heater, circuit breaker, and other household command centers. You can't always control where these are located—they might be completely spread out—so your job is to make sure they're always accessible. You'll need them in emergencies or when maintenance workers come through. Use rolling shelves if you can't avoid blocking them in.

332 CREATE A LIVING ZONE

If you have a finished section of your basement (maybe a media room or guest space), this is your living zone—somewhere the family gathers. It might also be a dedicated-use space, such as a play space, craft area, or workshop.

333 CREATE A STORAGE ZONE

If you're lucky enough to have an extra storage area in your basement, use it! The storage zone will divide into smaller zones as you categorize everything that remains after you purge unnecessary items. This is the space for furniture, bicycles, tools, and vacation or camping gear.

334 RETHINK FORGOTTEN SPACES

Utilize space that's often forgotten by adding storage in unexpected places. Try to think outside the box as to how odd solutions might work for you. If you've got stairs, install shelves underneath them to hold totes or bins. Some staircases may even have built-in closets or cupboards that can be put to all sorts of uses. For the ceiling, if you have enough space, use overhead racks and bins to get bulky items like artificial Christmas trees or bicycles out of the way. These also work for items that don't need to be readily accessible, like those sentimental clothes and books you're saving for your grandchildren. Don't forget about the walls—if you've ever tripped over a bike, you know that a wall-mounted bike rack is a great method for freeing up floor space.

335 KEEP BASEMENTS CLEAN AND DRY

After sorting your basement's contents and organizing everything that will be staying put for long-term storage, be smart about how you store these items. Use clear plastic containers that allow you to see what's inside, and set up a dehumidifier where possible—it will help control odors and prevent moisture buildup, which can damage your items. If you're storing furniture in the basement, drape drop cloths or blankets over them and keep them from touching the walls (which can harbor moisture). If you have an aboveground basement with windows and good air circulation, this may not be necessary. Follow your nose!

336 PRACTICE CAUTION WITH ARCHIVED ITEMS

You likely know someone who was greeted with ankle-deep water in the basement on the morning after a heavy rainstorm. Some areas are prone to flooding, and sometimes there's not much you can do about it—except protect your sentimental and valuable items. Don't set anything that could be harmed by water on the floor, and store any books, records, paper products, photos, textiles, or stuffed animals somewhere else (like the attic). If you need to put them in the basement, try ceiling-mounted racks with attachable bins, or keep them elevated with stacked cinder blocks. And stay away from cardboard containers!

QUICK TIP

MOUNT A FUSE-BOX FLASHLIGHT

You're bound to blow a fuse at some point, so grab some Velcro or magnetic tape and mount a flashlight right next to the fuse box. You'll know where to find it in the next blackout.

337 PERFECT YOUR PATIO

If you're lucky enough to have an outdoor space like a patio, porch, or deck for entertaining, it's time to get things in order to make sure you're ready. The perfect storage solution can sometimes be as simple as finding a new piece of multipurpose furniture to create spaces for things that previously didn't have an assigned home. If you grill often, repurpose a teak ladder as a shallow shelf and add hooks for BBQ implements or garden tools that need to be kept handy. Or use a wicker end table with a glass top to hold plants, drinks, and trays of food. A wall-mounted wire organizing rack can hold incoming mail on a front porch. Hide clutter with outdoor cabinets and storage units. There are endless options—find what works for your space.

338 GO VERTICAL

Even if you don't have a huge yard with lots of garden space, vertical patio gardening provides endless options and helps to avoid the traffic hazard that too many potted plants can cause. Incorporate vines, hanging plants, and mounted planter boxes along fences to open up walking paths and decorate the vertical surfaces.

QUICK TIP

USE THE PERIMETER

L-shaped benches against a wall will keep your guests comfortable while leaving the center space free for tables, fire pits, and grills.

339 INVEST IN OUTDOOR FABRICS

Outdoor furniture is built to withstand the elements, but be careful when choosing your cushions. Even if you don't sit outside very often, you'd be surprised what sun, rain, and general exposure to the elements can do to even the toughest fibers. Look for outdoor furniture–specific fabrics, which generally undergo a special chemical treatment to increase moisture resistance. If needed, hose fabrics down weekly, or deep-clean with a mild soap and water. Avoid detergents and hot water, which can compromise the protective materials. Store cushions in a covered area, and if they get caught in the rain, stand them on end to help them dry more quickly.

340 STASH CLEANING SUPPLIES OUTSIDE

Keeping outdoor surfaces consistently clean and clear helps prevent a huge cleaning project at the end of the summer. Store some cleaning products and rags in an outdoor-friendly bin for easy access to give surfaces a quick wipe down as needed.

341 COVER YOUR FIRE PIT

Over time, water and ash sitting in your fire pit can turn into lye and eat straight through its metal bottom. Luckily, this is easy to prevent. Once ashes cool, sweep them out of the pit. Alternatively, invest in a tight-fitting cover that can keep out the rain.

STOW OUTDOOR FURNITURE
AND CUSHIONS FOR THE WINTER

It can be a pain to clean and store outdoor furniture once the weather gets colder, but taking the time to do so will prevent weather damage and other wear and tear, adding years to the life of your furniture. Remember that outdoor furniture can be pricey—you'll be thankful for your hard work when you don't have to buy a new chaise lounge next year.

 # STORE SPLASH
SUPPLIES

If you have a pool or waterway nearby, you're likely stocked to the gills with floaties, toys, swimming aids, and other accessories. Mount hooks or wire baskets onto an old pallet or large piece of wood for a towel organization system that can move inside or outside as needed. Keep it in the garage or shed when not in use or during the off-season, and take it outside for the start of summer and pool parties. It can serve as a handy drying rack for wet suits and towels. It's also important to make sure any baskets or bins used for storage have good-sized holes or mesh in the bottom to drain water, and ensure your hooks (or any other places you store wet items) aren't too close together, so that air can circulate. The key to avoiding mildew is allowing air to get in and around items.

344 INSTALL SHELVING

The garage—or any utility space—can become a storage ground for clutter. Keep floors clear of items by installing vertical shelving systems or building your own. Choose from metal, wood, or plastic, but if you live in a humid area and your garage isn't insulated, watch out for the moisture that wood can absorb. Make sure to anchor all shelving into the wall studs to prevent accidents and injuries.

345 TAKE SHELVING TO THE TOP

Garage shelving doesn't need to feel fancy—inexpensive wire racks or makeshift plywood shelves will do the job. Because aesthetics aren't a top priority here, don't be afraid to build garage shelves up as high as you can. Store rarely used but necessary items on upper shelves, and keep more commonly used things toward the bottom.

346 CATEGORIZE AND CONTAINERIZE

A garage is a great place to store not only tools and automotive gear, but also off-season items like sports equipment, camping supplies, gardening tools, vacation essentials, and anything else that can be put away for a long period of time. Large totes fit well on most shelving units and can hold many things. Small containers are great for items such as rolls of adhesive, flashlights, tape measures, and other small tools. Categorize and containerize to keep your garage tidy.

347 UTILIZE THE CEILING

The ceiling is wasted space that most people don't think about incorporating into their garage storage. Hang bikes from utility hooks or add shelving over the garage door to store holiday decorations.

LABEL
EVERYTHING

Take organization one step further and label all containers, big and small. Use a label maker, hanging tags, chalkboard paint, or a vinyl lettering machine—whatever your preferred system might be. Labeling alleviates the need to search box after box to find what you're looking for. This can be especially useful in the garage, where things can go to live for a long time before they're sought after again.

UPDATE
FLOORING

Complete your garage overhaul by giving the floor a fresh coat of paint. Home improvement stores carry DIY garage floor painting kits so you can tackle it yourself. Or make it snappy and call in a professional.

350 FOLLOW THE SAFETY RULES

The garage can be a treacherous place, filled with all the flammable fuels, large machinery, and sharp tools that we don't want to keep in the house. Keep your lawn mower, weed whacker, and other machinery (and tripping hazards like rakes) away from kid-friendly zones and high-traffic pathways. Store flammables and chemicals according to directions. Read warning labels carefully. Chemicals and paint should be secured away from children. Store sharps out of reach of children. Always keep dangerous chemicals in their original containers. Always keep a working fire extinguisher in the garage. They expire, so be sure to check the date, mark your calendar, and replace it when needed. You'll also want to install a carbon monoxide detector.

QUICK TIP

STORE TOOLS

There are many ways to sort your tool storage. Mount a pegboard on the wall to neatly display tools and tidbits. Add a coat of spray paint and trim for a more custom look. Use classic mason jars for smaller items—they're perfect for just about any type of project. Put nails and screws on display, feed twine through a hole in a lid, or store a dozen sticks of glue—the sky's the limit! Last but not least, stackable, clear shoeboxes can store all types of tools, sharps (such as box cutters), and other handy items.

351 STORE SPORTS GEAR

Rig up a few bungee cords to create a ball storage system, or throw basketballs into a net that cinches at the top. Get bats, rackets, clubs, sticks, and other gear off the floor and onto the wall using hooks or brackets.

352 STORE UNTIL WINTER

Keep snow boots, shovels, holiday decorations, and sidewalk salt in a designated area. Make sure breakable items are carefully wrapped and secured inside labeled plastic bins. Always place larger and heavier items on the bottom of a stack and lighter bins on top. And remember that overloading containers can lead to dropping them!

353 GET THE HOLIDAY HOOKUP

Wrap Christmas lights, tinsel, and other tangle-prone garlands around plastic hangers or sturdy pieces of cardboard before putting them into storage for the next eleven months. You'll thank yourself later when trimming your tree doesn't get delayed by an hour-long detangling party. You can also buy holiday-light storage reels to serve the same purpose. If you have multiple sets, label each garland with its destination to save time (for example, "banister," "porch column," "front tree"). For ornaments, store small ones in egg cartons (the sturdy plastic kind are best) or apple crates. Old wine and beer crates are great for storing larger ornaments. After the holiday is over, make a list of things you need to buy next year. Better yet, run out and grab them now! Those post-holiday markdowns can't be beat.

KEEP
CLEAN

It takes a little extra effort to keep garages and other areas that see a lot of outdoor activity clean and protected from the elements. Sweep floors with a push broom and wipe down sills and frames to keep cobwebs at bay. Clean screens with warm water and all-purpose cleaner, using a scrub brush to get into the mesh as well as the frames. Then hose them off and allow to air dry. If you have a large deck or porch, or a drain in your garage, a power washer can be a great investment for blasting away mildew, dirt, and stains—just be sure not to use it on untreated wood. Watch for loose nails, fill holes with putty, and make sure to reseal your deck and floors when needed. Wash light fixture covers every month, as insects tend to collect inside, and dry thoroughly before you replace them.

CREATE A
GOODBYE STATION

Set up a "goodbye" station in your garage for any items that are on their way out. This will help you keep track of these items and remind you to take them to their assigned new homes. Separate them as follows:

DONATE: Items you are donating

RETURN: Store-bought items that need to be returned—make it a mission to return them all within a week!

SELL: Anything that you will be selling in your upcoming garage sale

BORROWED: Items that need to return to their rightful owners

356 ADD A TRASH CAN

Maintaining a clean car can seem impossible when we have crazy, busy days—or, of course, kids! Use a small or medium trash bag to line a large plastic cereal dispenser (with a lid). Keep it in the car to use as a trash can. The lid prevents trash from spilling out and making a mess, and it's way better than garbage being spread across the entire back seat. Empty the bag every evening.

EMPTY THE CAR OUT

The number one way to keep the car tidy is to empty it out completely every time you return home. Make it part of the routine for the whole family, and teach kids to be responsible for removing their own things.

358

ELIMINATE UNNECESSARY CLUTTER

Take an inventory of everything that's being kept in the car full time. Is it all being used? Remove anything that isn't a functional part of traveling. By removing excess items, the car will stay tidy.

359

VACUUM AND CLEAN YOUR CAR

Take pride in your car—there's a good chance you spent a fortune on it! And a sparkly clean car feels as good as a clean house, with much less work. Vacuum, clean the windows, and wipe down the interior regularly.

360

ACCOMMODATE QUICK CLEANING

Convenient, portable cleaning supplies, like wet wipes and a microfiber duster, can make all the difference when it comes to keeping your car feeling fresh. If you're waiting in the car for even a small amount of time, make the most of those few minutes by wiping down your dashboard and doing some quick dusting. Making these small cleaning tasks into a regular practice can save you time during a seasonal deep clean.

361 HACK THE CUPHOLDER

Between dust, crumbs, and other foods spills, cupholders can be tedious to clean. Place silicone cupcake liners in your car's cupholders to create a barrier against hard-to-clean messes. Once they are dirty, remove the cupcake holders, give them a wash, and return them to the car.

362 KEEP THE GLOVE BOX UNDER CONTROL

From old insurance stubs to mechanic receipts, the glove box attracts paper clutter like a magnet. Clear out papers you don't need and place important items, such as your registration and proof of insurance, in a plastic sheet protector or a folder. When your new car registration and insurance come in the mail, swap out the old paperwork immediately. Your car manual and other important car reference materials should be the only other papers inside.

363

STOCK THE CAR FOR EMERGENCIES

While on the go, you're bound to run into a few accidents or emergencies. Prepare ahead of time by putting together emergency kits for the car. You never know when a need will arise, so it's best to be ready for the unexpected. Just remember to remove temperature-sensitive items from the car during periods or seasons of extreme heat or cold.

EMERGENCY KIT
- Personal care kit (hand sanitizer, tisues, tampons and pads, lip balm, lotion, sunscreen, trash bag, water bottle, blanket, extra money, nonperishable snacks)
- First aid kit
- Potty training kit (wipes, extra clothing diapers, pull-ups, plastic bag)

CAR CARE KIT
- Jumper cables
- Flashlight and extra batteries
- Duct tape
- Multipurpose utility tool
- Flare lights
- Tire sealant
- Gloves
- Tow rope
- Shovel

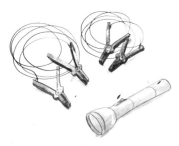

364

SORT THE TRUNK INTO BINS

Keeping a few plastic bins in your trunk will help you keep the space organized, no matter what you're transporting, from sports equipment to camping supplies to groceries. Consider including a few empty bins so you have additional storage on hand if necessary.

365   CONSIDER A NO-SNACKS RULE

It sounds harsh, but if your family leaves behind trash or other messes after they snack in the car, it might be smart to make the car a food-free zone. You'll avoid the constant buildup of crumbs, wrappers, and spills. Of course, exceptions can be made for certain occasions like road trips, but on a day-to-day basis, it will make a huge difference.

INDEX

weldon**owen**

an imprint of Insight Editions
P.O. Box 3088
San Rafael, CA 94912
www.weldonowen.com

Follow us on Facebook:
www.facebook.com/weldonowen/

Follow us on Twitter:
@WeldonOwen

Follow us on Instagram:
weldonowen

CEO Raoul Goff
VP PUBLISHER Roger Shaw
EDITORIAL DIRECTOR Katie Killebrew
VP MANUFACTURING Alix Nicholaeff
ART DIRECTOR Allister Fein
PROJECT EDITOR Claire Yee
PRODUCTION MANAGER Sam Taylor

Weldon Owen would also like to thank Caylin
Harris, Allie Kiekhofer, Anna Embree, and
Kevin Broccoli.

ISBN: 978-1-68188-835-4

Printed in Turkey by Elma Basim

First printed in 2022

2025 2024 2023 2022
10 9 8 7 6 5 4 3 2 1

CREDITS

All photos from Shutterstock unless
otherwise noted.

All illustrations courtesy of Louise
Morgan except the following: Juan Calle:
002, 017, 052, 070, 118